** The Gate of Unity - Shaar HaYichud **

Gate #1 of Chovot Halevavot - Duties of the Heart
by Rabeinu Bahya ibn Paquda zt'l
(with commentaries)

english translation by Rabbi Yosef Sebag

yosefsebag@gmail.com

Original Hebrew at end of book

Dafyomi Advancement Forum

Produced by Kollel Iyun Hadaf • Rosh Kollel: Rabbi Mordecai Kornfeld

'Your Chavrusa in Yerushalayim'

בס"ד

Chovos ha'Levavos, the monumental work of Rabeinu Bachye ben Yosef Ibn Pakuda, a judge in Islamic Spain (circa 1040), is one of the earliest works on Jewish philosophy and beliefs. It remains one of the fundamental works of Musar and Hashkafah. Even the great Rambam (Maimonides) bases a large part of his treatises in these fields on the revered words of the Chovos ha'Levavos. (It has been suggested that Rav Shlomo Ibn Gevirol took ideas from the Chovos ha'Levavos as well.)

Originally written in Arabic, this classic was translated into Hebrew not longer after its original publication, and more recently to many other languages. Among works of Jewish philosophy, its prominence in even the most traditional houses of learning makes it unique. The Chovos ha'Levavos' methodical and systematic analyses or every aspect of the human character makes reading it an experience in growth through introspection.

We owe a debt of gratitude to Rabbi Yosef Sebag for his exceptionally readable English translation of this important work. By adding translations of classic commentaries on the text, he has made the depth of the work available to all. Rabbi Sebag's investment of time and effort is evident in every part of the work, but especially in the Sha'ar ha'Yichud, the somewhat "controversial" section dealing with philosophical proofs of G-d.

I have known Rabbi Sebag for many years, and I have witnessed firsthand his overwhelming dedication to Torah-study and to raising a family on Torah-true ideals. His careful adherence to the instructions of our Torah giants, coupled with his strong will to teach others the timeless lessons of the Torah, has made him a true "Ben Aliyah."

May his investment bear the dividends of allowing him to help many of our brethren improve their faith and strength of character!

With Torah blessings,

Mordecai Kornfeld

Rabbi Mordecai Kornfeld

Israel office: P.O.B. 43087, Jerusalem 91430, Israel • US office: 140-32 69 Ave., Flushing, NY 11367
Tel. - Israel: (02) 651-5004 • Fax - Israel: (02) 591-6024 • email: daf@dafyomi.co.il
http://www.dafyomi.co.il • http://dafyomi.shemayisrael.co.il/
U.S. tax ID: 11-3354586   580-28-908-0 ע"ר מס'

** Shaar HaYichud - Gate of Unity of G-d **

(with commentaries)
from Chovos Halevavos - Duties of the Heart
by Rabeinu Bahya ibn Paquda zt'l
(originally published 1080 CE)

english translation by Rabbi Yosef Sebag

Important Foreword:

This treatise sets out to demonstrate through rational investigation that this world must have a Creator who created it from nothing and that it is impossible otherwise. In doing so, it also provides a fascinating introduction to G-d. Many of the philosophical arguments used have been revised and reformulated over the generations. Thus, the terminology and methodology of these proofs may seem antiquated or outdated even though they remain philosophically sound.

There is a difference of opinion among the Torah authorities as to whether this section should be studied by the typical student of the Torah. Many Torah luminaries maintain that one should not seek philosophical proofs of G-d's existence. Belief in G-d should be based on the Mesorah (Tradition) that we received from our elders and mentors, the study of G-d's wondrous Torah, and the many ways He manifests Himself in His creations and in our daily lives. Indeed as the Pas Lechem commentary writes at the start of the next gate: "In philosophical inquiry, a man is not assured from stumbling and erring in treading this path, as in truth, there are many, many casualties strewn along the path of philosophical inquiry..."

For this reason, I have tried to add commentaries to provide a basic, but probably insufficient amount of guidance. If something does not make sense, please investigate with a wise Rabbi first before drawing the wrong conclusions. Also keep in mind, that it is important to study it in its entirety as many concluding points in the end tie everything together.

I once heard Rabbi Zev Leff say in a lecture: "in the time of the Rambam people were really seeking, and bringing intellectual proofs was beneficial, but today the biggest question on people's minds is whether to put ketchup or mustard on their hotdogs". Tragically most people have become comfortable living superficially, content to spend their few dozen years of life without thinking of who they are and why they are here. It is my hope that this translation will arouse others and myself on these questions.

In translating this, I consulted with the classic hebrew commentaries and also the out of print translation by Rabbi Moses Hyamson which came to my possession in a miraculous way. The translator studied in various yeshivas under great Torah scholars such as Rabbi Dov Shwartzman zt'l (~2 years), Rabbi Nachman Bulman zt'l, Rabbi Nissan Kaplan (~5 years). He also completed a degree in physics at the University of Massachusetts, Amherst and was a research associate in nuclear physics for a few years before heading off to yeshiva.

- Yosef Sebag, Jerusalem, June 2015 - Sivan 5775

Abbreviations used in this translation:
MH - Manoach HeLevavos commentary by Rabbi Manoach Hendel (1540-1611)
TL - Tov HaLevanon commentary by Rabbi Yisrael Halevi (1700-1777)
PL - Pas Lechem commentary by Rabbi Chaim Avraham Hacohen (1740-1815)
ML - Marpe Lenefesh commentary by Rabbi Refael Mendel (1825-1895)
LT - Lev Tov commentary by Rabbi Pinchas Lieberman (1929-2005)

*** INTRODUCTION ***

The author says:

After investigating after what is the most necessary of the cornerstones and fundamentals of our religion, we found that the wholehearted acceptance of the unity of G-d is the root and foundation of Judaism. It is the first of the gates of the Torah, and it differentiates between the believer and the heretic. It is the head and front of religious truth, and one who strays from it - will not be able to perform religious deeds and his faith will not endure.

> (some commentaries:
> even if he does good deeds, his acts will not be correct and built on a foundation, nor will they be whole and enduring and if there is no foundation, the entire building will eventually collapse - *Pas Lechem*
> "he will not have any merit for his religious deeds" - Tov Halevanon
> "he will not be able to perform the service of G-d, since if one does not believe in Him, that He created the world, and that He is alone in His world, and that it is befitting to serve Him, if so, one has no master that he should serve, and there's no greater non-believer than this" - *Manoach Levavos*)

Because of this, G-d's first words to us at Mount Sinai were: "I am the L-ord your G-d...you shall not have other gods before Me", and later on He exhorted us through His prophet saying: (Shema Yisrael..) *"Hear O Israel the L-ord, is our G-d, the L-ord is One"* (Deut. 6:4)

You should study this chapter of Shema Yisrael until its close, and you will see how its words move from one matter to another, encompassing 10 matters, that number corresponding to the Ten Commandments. The explanation is as follows:

First there is the command to believe in the Creator, when it says *"Hear O Israel the L-ord"*. His intent was not for hearing of the ear, but rather for belief and acceptance of the heart, as the verse says *"we will do and we will hear" (Ex. 24:7)*, and *"Hear therefore, O Israel, and observe to do it" (Deut. 6:3)*, and similarly for all other verses which come in this way using a term denoting "hearing", the intent is only to bring to belief and acceptance.

After He placed us under obligation to believe in the reality of His existence (through rational investigation for those capable as in ch.3), we are then called upon to believe that He is our G-d, as indicated in the word "our G-d", and afterwards He commanded us to believe that He [alone] is truly one, in saying: "G-d is one" .

> (*Marpe Lenefesh*: "G-d is one" - that only G-d is truly one, but nothing else is truly one under any circumstances, and even if we say on something that it is "one", it is not really one, except in passing (relatively), rather it is more than one as will be explained.
>
> *Tov Halevanon*: If the intent in saying "one" was merely to exclude multiple gods, it should have said "H-shem yachid" (which, in hebrew, connotes specifically one and not many)...
> "our G-d" - He granted us existence and formed us, and took us to be His people.
>
> *Marpe Lenefesh*: "our G-d" - this eternal Being, who reigns supreme over all worlds, even so, He is specifically "our G-d", for He chose us among all nations during the giving of the Torah to be His treasured nation, and He drew us near to His service, and we undertook His sovereignty over us.
>
> *Translator*: "After He placed us under obligation to believe in (1) the reality of His existence, we are then (2) called upon to believe that He is our G-d" - The two blessings before reciting the Shema also correspond to these two aspects. The theme of the first blessing is knowing G-d through His creating this vast universe and the mystical worlds, etc. While the theme of the second blessing is that He is our G-d in having chosen us and giving us the Torah, etc.)

After He bid us to believe and accept these three principles we mentioned, He proceeded to what is incumbent on us to follow them with, namely, to love G-d wholeheartedly, in private and in public, with our life and with our might, as He said: *"And you shall love the L-ord your G-d with all your heart, and with all your soul, and with all your might" (Deut. 6:5)*. I intend to clarify this matter in the Gate of Love of G-d (Gate #10), with the Al-mighty's help.

Afterwards, He moved on to exhort on the duties of the heart, in saying: *"And these words, which I command you this day, shall be on your heart"*, which means to cleave them to your heart, and believe them in your inner being.

Afterwards, He proceeded to the commandments of the limbs which require both thought and action, as He said: "you shall teach them to your sons".

> (this refers to Torah study, which requires understanding of the heart (mind) and also physical acts, namely moving of the lips and pronunciation of the tongue - *PL*
> He started with the commandments of the limbs which are most important and most central, namely those which employ the mouth and tongue combined with the heart - to learn and teach Torah and to recite the Shema.)

And so that if you don't have a son, you will not mistakenly think that the (commandment of) verbally reading depends on having a son, He said: "You shall speak in them".

> (that on oneself is the primary obligation to study Torah - *TL*, another commentary: Do not think that since the main purpose is understanding of the heart, if so, the need for verbally speaking it with one's mouth is only for making them known to the sons, therefore he said that even by oneself one needs to verbally pronounce them with one's mouth and tongue - *PL*)

Afterwards, He continued: *"and you shall speak in them when you sit in your house, and when you walk by the way, and when you lie down, and when you rise up"*, because the heart and tongue are never prevented from fulfilling the duties which apply to them, unlike the other limbs (which depend on various times and circumstances). In the introduction of this book, we have already pointed out that the duties of the heart are a constant duty.

And the purpose of all of this is to exhort on what He said previously: *"And these words, which I command you this day, shall be on your heart"*, which means that habitually having them on one's tongue always, brings to remembrance of the heart, and to never turn one's heart away from always remembering G-d, and this is similar to what King David, peace be unto him, said: *"I have set the L-ord always before me" (Tehilim 16:8)*. And scripture says: *"But the word is very near unto you, in your mouth, and in your heart, that you may do it" (Deut. 30:14)*.

(*Marpe Lenefesh:* because this is the primary goal of all the levels of the Tzadikim (righteous) and the Chasidim (pious) - to not empty one's heart from remembering G-d always, as the Rama says in the first halacha in the Shulchan Aruch, which are the words of the Morey Nevuchim (Maimonides' Guide for the Perplexed) part 3 chapter 52, see there, and see also later on, and the Sefer Chasidim siman 35.

Tov Halevanon: The reason the Torah exhorted on doing this always even though it is not an obligation to do this always, on this the author answered that the intent of the verse is on habituating the tongue on them always...)

Afterwards, He proceeded to the duties of the limbs which consist of action only, and gave three examples, as He said: *"And you shall bind them for a sign upon your hand; And they shall be as Totafot between your eyes; And you shall write them upon the doorposts of your house, and on your gates"*, which refers to the Tefilin of the hand and of the head, and the Mezuza, all of whom cause one to remember the Creator, and to wholeheartedly love Him, and yearn to Him, and as scripture says regarding how lovers keep their love in mind: *"Set me as a seal upon your heart, as a seal upon your arm"* (Songs 8:6), and *"Behold, I have engraved you upon the palms of my hands"* (Isaiah 49:16), and *"In that day, says the L-ord of hosts, will I take you, O Zerubavel, my servant, the son of Shealtiel, says the L-ord, and will make you as a signet ring: for I have chosen you"* (Chagai 2:23), and *"A bundle of myrrh is my beloved unto me; it (the myrrh) shall lie between my breasts"* (Songs 1:13). G-d ordained three signs in order that they be stronger and more enduring, as the wise man said: *"a threefold cord is not quickly broken"* (Eccles. 4:12).

(*Manoach Halevavos:* "he (the myrrh) shall lie between my breasts" - this hints to the heart, which is between the breasts. The author renders the verse as referring to the practice of a man's beloved to give him a bundle of myrrh to hang around his neck, until it reaches between his breasts. Thus he remembers his beloved always since the fragrance continuously rises to his nostrils from between his breasts, and he keeps the beloved in mind. The hint is to the precepts, which were given to us in order to remember G-d always, such as Tefilin, Tzitzit etc.)

Hence, this chapter contains ten matters, five of them concern the spiritual (mind/heart), and five of them the physical (the body).

The 5 spiritual: (1) That the Creator exists. (2) He is our G-d. (3) He is the true Unity. (4) That we love Him with all our heart. (5) That we serve Him wholeheartedly.

The 5 physical: (1) You shall teach them to your children. (2) You shall speak in them (3) You shall bind them as a sign on your hand (4) They shall be as Totafot between your eyes. (5) You shall write them upon the doorposts of your house and upon your gates.

And our Rabbis taught: "why does the reciting of the chapter 'Hear O Israel' precede the reciting of the chapter "And it shall be..."? (i.e.the second chapter. answer:) To teach that one must first acknowledge the sovereignty of G-d and afterwards assume the duty to fulfill His commandments" (Berachot 13a). Therefore, I deemed it proper to precede the Gate of Unity to the other gates of this book.

It will now be necessary for me to clarify on the subject of wholeheartedly acknowledging the unity (of G-d) ten matters:
1. What is the definition of the wholehearted acceptance of G-d's unity?
2. how many divisions does the subject of unity divide into?
3. whether or not it is our duty to intellectually investigate the matter.
4. what is the manner of investigating it and which introductions must we know before we investigate the unity?
5. To clarify the premises which demonstrate that the world has a Creator who created it from nothing.
6. how we apply them to establish the existence of the Creator.
7. to bring proofs that He is one.
8. to clarify the matter of a conventional (relative) unity versus a true unity.
9. demonstration that G-d alone is the true Unity and that there is no

true Unity besides Him.

10. the Divine attributes, those deduced by reason and those written in scripture and the ways in which these should be ascribed to G-d or denied to Him.

*** CHAPTER 1 ***

The definition of the wholehearted acceptance of the unity of G-d is that the heart and the tongue are equal in acknowledging the unity of G-d, after understanding, in the way of logical proofs, the certainty of His existence and the truth of His unity. For acknowledgement of the unity of G-d among men differs according to their level of intelligence and understanding.

(*Marpe Lenefesh*: the meaning of the word "definition" is: "a correct and complete teaching on the thing that one wishes to explain what it is". Therefore one must call it with a name which is specific to it, so that the reader does not err that one's intent was for something else... for example, if we define a human being as a "speaking being" - this is a comprehensive teaching without breaches, but if you define him as an "alive being" - this is not a complete definition, and there is a breach in your words since animals are also called "alive". So too for all things similar to this. Understand this. Now, likewise for the matter of the unity of the Creator, when the tongue and the heart are equal, and a person understands by the ways of logical proofs, that which a person says of the Creator that He is "One", how He is One, then the person's unifying (G-d) in his heart is a complete teaching on G-d, but if the person cannot bring logical proofs, and he says on G-d that He is "one", this is not a complete teaching on G-d, and there is a breach in his words, because there are many things in the world which are also called "one", even though they are not truly one, since really they are more than one, as will be explained. With this introduction you will understand this chapter and the next.)

Among them: One who declares the unity (of G-d) with only his tongue, namely, that he hears people say something and he is drawn after them without understanding the meaning of what he is saying.

Among them: One who declares the unity of G-d with his heart and tongue, who understands the matter of what he is saying through the Tradition that he received from his ancestors, but he does not understand the clarification of what he received of this matter, and the truth of what he believes in this matter.

Among them: One who declares His unity after understanding through logical proofs the truth of the matter, but he will conceive G-d's Unity like other unities to be found, and he will come to form a material conception of the Creator and represent Him with a form and likeness because he does not understand the true nature of His Unity and the matter of His existence.

Among them: One who declares G-d's unity with his heart and with his tongue after understanding the concept of true unity versus relative unity, and he can bring proofs to demonstrate G-d's existence and true Unity - this class of men is the complete (unblemished) group regarding the matter of unity of G-d.

Therefore, I defined the wholehearted acknowledgement of the unity (of G-d) - that it is the equalizing of the tongue and the heart (mind)) in the unity of the Creator, after one knows how to bring proofs on it and understands the ways of His true Unity through rational investigation.

*** CHAPTER 2 ***

> (*Marpe Lenefesh*: Now he will explain from where came these different outlooks regarding the unity of G-d mentioned in chapter 1, he answers: since this word became common language and became used in their other affairs and needs.)

The author says: Regarding how many ways the unity of the Creator is conceived, I will answer as follows: Since the word "unity" spread among men of the unity (Jews), they became accustomed to using it frequently in their tongue and speech, until it became an expression of amazement whether for good or for bad.

> (when some unusual amazing matter occurs to them whether good or bad, they will say it is a singular and unique matter, with no equal in the way of exaggeration and singling out - *TL*)

And they use it to express their dread of great calamity, and to exaggerate it and to express amazement on it, and they don't put to heart to understand the true matter of what passes through their tongue (when reciting the Shema), due to ignorance and laziness. And they consider the matter of Unity is done for them when they finish (reciting) its words, and they do not sense that their heart is devoid of His truth and that their mind is empty of its meaning because they declare His unity with their tongue and in words. They will conceive Him in their hearts to be more than One (i.e. with forms of "plurality" as will be explained) and represent Him in their minds with the likeness of other "unities" to be found, and they will speak of His attributes in a way that cannot belong to the true Unity (such as women and the masses who attribute to G-d love, hate, and anger as they imagine it in human beings - *PL*), because they don't understand the matter of true Unity versus temporary unity, except for a treasured few who plumbed the depths of wisdom and understood the matter of the Creator versus the created, and the characteristics of true Unity and what G-d is singular in.

The philosopher spoke truth when he said: "no one can serve the Cause of causes and Beginning of beginnings except the prophet of the generation with his senses or the primary (perfect - TL) philosopher with the wisdom he acquired, but others serve other than Him, since they cannot conceive what exists (without beginning

- *TL*), but rather can only conceive that which is composite (i.e. created things - *TL*).

> *Marpe Lenefesh*: It is known that the prophets see, hear, and apprehend with their supernatural spiritual eyes as if they saw and heard them with their physical senses - awesome things which the philosophers and Sages would squander most of their lives to try to grasp correctly, and it is possible that they never manage to grasp them correctly, as the Kuzari book spoke on this.
>
> *Translator*: Many people mistakenly think the proofs of G-d have been refuted in our times. But these "refutations" are mistakenly based on treating the Eternal with the same logic as the non-eternal. It is not at all obvious what is implied by Eternal, as we will see.

Because of this the acceptance of the Unity falls into four divisions, corresponding to the different levels of recognition and understanding in men:

(1) Unity of G-d in the tongue only. This level is reached by the child and the simpleton who does not understand the matter of (true) religion, and in whose heart its truth is not fixed.

(2) Unity of G-d in the mind and in the tongue through Tradition, because he believes those who he received from, but he does not understand the truth of the matter through his own intellect and understanding. He is like the blind man who follows the seeing man, and it is possible that the one he follows received the Tradition from a receiver like himself, whereby it would be like a procession of blind men where each one places his hands on the shoulders of the fellow before him until at the head is a seeing man who guides them all. If the seeing man fails them or neglects them and is not careful to guard them, or if one of the blind men in the chain stumbles or some other trouble happens - all of them will share the same fate, and will stray from the path; and it is possible they will fall in a pit or ditch, or they will stumble in something which blocks their progress.

> (*Tov Halevanon commentary*: Certainly for a blind man who leans on a seeing man, it is impossible that he will align his walking very straight like the seeing man, without straying a

bit in his steps. And even though this is not perceivable in the first blind man who is close to the seeing man, nevertheless, if there are many blind men who follow the seeing man, then, when each of them strays a bit, the combined straying will accumulate until it is possible that one of them will stumble. Furthermore, all of them will deviate from the straight path. The analogy is that one who does not know the truth of faith through his own intellect but instead relies on tradition, one man from another, for many generations up until the one who properly understood from his intellect, behold, most of the time, it is possible that each one strayed a bit from the truth, until eventually, it became a big straying...)

Similarly for one who proclaims the unity out of tradition, one cannot be sure he will not come to association (which is the opposite of unity - PL), that if he hears the words of the Meshanim and their claims, It is possible that he will change his outlook, and will err without noticing. Because of this our Sages said: *"Be eager to study the Torah and know what to respond to an apikoros (heretic)"* (Pirkei Avos 2:14).

(*Tov Halevanon*: there was a man called Mani, yimach shemo, who would claim there are two gods, one who does good and one who does evil, and those who went after him are called after his name with the term: Minim. The word "apikoros" refers to the name of a man who was called "apikoros", yimach shemo, who would completely deny the existence of G-d, the Moray (Maimonides' guide for the perplexed) mentions him in the end of the first chapter, those drawn after his views are called "apikorsim", this term was also borrowed to refer to those who denigrate the Sages, and falsely give misinterpretations of the Torah, or the like, as brought in tractate Sanhedrin)

(3) The third group: Unity of G-d with the mind and the tongue after one can bring logical proofs demonstrating the truth of His existence, but without understanding the matter of true Unity versus temporary unity. This is like a seeing man who is travelling along the road, wishing to reach a faraway land. Even though he knows the general direction, but the road splits to many uncertain roads, and he does not recognize the correct road which leads to the city he

wishes to reach.

> (*Marpe Lenefesh*: he knows without doubt through logical proofs that there is a Being who created the world and that there is no other G-d, but he does not know the difference between the Creator and His creations.
>
> *Translator*: his awe of the greatness of G-d will be weak, therefore his worship will be mostly by rote and without zeal. Hence, he will not get far.)

He will greatly tire himself and will fail to reach his destination, because he does not know the (correct) road, as the verse says: "the toil of the fool will tire him who knows not to reach a city" (Eccles. 10:15).

> (*Tov Halevanon*: The term "fool" applies to a man who is able to understand with his faculties, however, he does not want to toil but instead seeks comfort, as in *"the fool does not desire understanding"* (Mishlei 18:2), this is what the verse says:
> *"the toil of the fool"* - meaning the toil that the fool fears from and instead chooses comfort for himself.
> *"will tire him"* - Just the opposite, it will tire him even more.
> *"who knows not to reach a city"* - Just like he is lazy to study the roads properly, thinking he will manage without knowing it well, he will tire himself even more, because he will bring himself to err on the road and will not reach any city.
>
> Pas Lechem: he is called a fool because he did not investigate and inquire which roads to take before setting on the journey. He is the opposite of the wise man, who looks into the future, whose eyes are on the head of every matter to contemplate beforehand every matter [and its consequences].)

(4) The fourth group: Acknowledgement of the Unity of G-d with the mind and the tongue after one knows how to bring proofs on it, and to comprehend the truth of His Unity through intellectual derivation and correct, sound reasoning - this is the complete and important group, and this is the level which the prophet exhorted us in saying: "Know therefore this day, and set it in your heart, that the L-ord He

is G-d" (Deut. 4:39).

*** CHAPTER 3 ***

Regarding whether or not it is our duty to rationally investigate on the unity of G-d, I will say as follows: For anyone who is capable of investigating on this and other similar matters through rational inquiry - it is his duty to do so according to his intelligence and perception.

I have already written in the introduction to this book sufficient arguments which demonstrate the obligation of this matter. Anyone who neglects to investigate into it is blameworthy and is considered as belonging to the class of men who fall short in wisdom and conduct (because there are things which touch on practical matters as clarified in the introduction - *PL*). He is like a sick man (a doctor) who is an expert on the nature of his disease and the correct healing method, but instead relies on another doctor to heal him who applies various healing methods, while he is lazy to inquire using his own wisdom and reasoning into the methods employed by the doctor, to see whether or not the doctor is dealing with him correctly or not, when he was easily able to do this without anything preventing him. The Torah has already obligated us on this, as written: "know therefore today, and lay it to your heart[, that the L-ord is G-d in heaven above and on the earth beneath; there is no other]" (Deut. 4:39).

The proof that "lay it to your heart" refers to intellectual investigation, is from what the following verse says: "And none lays it to his heart, neither is there knowledge nor understanding" (Isaiah 44:19). So too David urged his son: "And you, Solomon my son, *know you* the G-d of your father, and serve him with a perfect heart and with a willing soul; for the L-ord searches all hearts" (Chronicles 28:9).

> (*Pas Lechem*: Through knowing G-d with your intellect, your heart will be perfect and your soul will be willing in His service. This is the meaning of "and serve him with a perfect heart and with a willing soul".

And David said: "*Know you* that the L-ord He is G-d" (Ps. 100:3).

> (*Pas Lechem*: "*the L-ord He is G-d*" - this is the primary matter of the Unity - to know that even though He exhibits

different actions such as mercy and justice, nevertheless, in His essence, He has no plurality, rather the L-ord (His Name of mercy) is G-d (Elokim, His Name of justice)...

And "Because he has set his love upon Me, therefore will I deliver him: I will set him on high, because he has *known* My Name" (Ps. 91:14), and "But let him that glories glory in this, that he understands and *knows* Me" (Yirmiya 9:23), and our Sages said: "be diligent in the study of Torah and know what to answer a heretic" (Avos 2:14), and the Torah says: "Keep therefore and do them; for this is your wisdom and your understanding in the sight of the nations.." (Deut. 4:6).

And it is impossible for the nations to admit to our claims of superior wisdom and understanding unless there are proofs and evidences which can testify for us along with the testimony of the intellect on the truth of our Torah and our faith. And our Maker has already promised us that He will remove the veil of ignorance from their minds, and show His magnificent glory as a sign to us on the truth of our Torah when He said: "And the nations shall walk by your light" (Isaiah 60:3), and "And many peoples shall go and say, Come you, and let us go up to the mountain of the L-ord, to the house of the G-d of Jacob.." (Isaiah 2:3).

(*Marpe Lenefesh*: He wrote this point so that you would not wonder, "behold, here are all the proofs and evidences, and the testimony of the intellect and the tradition are faithfully in our hands, which they are not capable of refuting, and they still do not retract from their error??".. For this he said that the "veil of ignorance", which refers to the overpowering of the lusts of this world (over their intellect)..as explained in the Gate of Abstinence... it is what separates between them and the truth, that they will not recognize it until G-d removes from them the veil of ignorance from the face of their intellect)

It is now clear from logic, scripture, and tradition that it is our duty to investigate into this of what we are capable of clearly grasping with our minds.

*** CHAPTER 4 ***

Regarding what is the way to investigate on the truth of the unity, and what introductions we need to know before we investigate on this unity, I will say as follows.

Any matter which one would like to understand when one is in doubt of its very existence, must first ask "does it exist or not?" After one has established its existence, one must then enquire as to what it is, how it is, and why it is. But regarding the Creator, a man may only ask whether He exists. And when His existence is demonstrated through rational investigation, we may further enquire whether He is one or more than one. And when it is clear that He is one, we may enquire on the matter of unity, and on how many ways this term is used, and in this way we will establish for ourselves the complete recognition of the unity of G-d, as the verse says: *"Hear O Israel, the L-ord is our G-d, the L-ord is One"* (Deut. 6:4).

Therefore, we must first enquire whether or not this world has a Creator. When it becomes clear that the world has a Creator who created it as something new, we can then further enquire whether He is one or more than one. Then, when it will be established that He is one, we can investigate into the matter of true (absolute) Unity and temporary (relative) unity, and then consider what we can say of the Creator regarding His true matter, and through this we will have completed the matter of acknowledgement of the unity of G-d in our hearts and minds, with G-d's help.

*** CHAPTER 5 ***

> INTRODUCTION TO LOGICAL PROOFS (excerpt from Gate 5)
>
> *Tov Halevanon*: It is known that through two ways a [logical] proof is established. One, through true premises. Two, through conclusions that necessarily follow. i.e. if there is a foundation of premises which are undoubtedly true, then when the premises are combined with each other, the conclusions that are drawn from them must undoubtedly follow... a spurious and faulty proof is due to either one of the premises is not true or that the conclusion does not follow these premises on proper consideration.
>
> *Pas Lechem*: For example, if we start with the premise that Reuven is taller than Shimon and Shimon is taller than Levi. Then the conclusion that necessarily follows is that Reuven is taller than Levi. However, it is possible that the premises are not true, that Reuven is not taller than Shimon or that Shimon is not taller than Levi, and the conclusions are automatically null and void. The second example, if we establish that Reuven loves Shimon and Shimon loves Levi, and we want to draw the conclusion that Reuven loves Levi. Even though the premises are true, the conclusion does not necessarily follow.

There are three premises which lead to the inference that this world has a Creator who created it from nothing:
1) A thing cannot make itself.
2) Beginnings (causes) are limited in number; therefore, they must have a First Beginning (First cause) which had no beginning (cause) before it.
3) Anything composite must have been brought into existence (cannot be eternal, i.e. without beginning).

When these three premises are established, the inference will be, for one who understands how to apply them and combine them - that the world has a Creator who created it from nothing, as we will demonstrate with G-d's help.

> (*Tov Halevanon commentary*: Understand, that to clarify the roots of religion, there are many different ways, but the

central pillar which everything depends on is the logical demonstration of the "chidush haolam" (this world was brought into existence from nothing). When this has been clarified, then automatically, it will be demonstrated the existence of G-d who created it. Many of our Sages already endeavored in this route such as Rabeinu Saadia Gaon, and Rambam (Maimonides). Behold, Rambam in part 1 chapter 73 of the Moray Nevuchim started to show the logical demonstration of the existence of G-d and that He is the absolute Unity and not physical, but he brought the proofs from the words of the philosophers, and he spoke at length denigrating their views and all of their proofs. He then returned at the beginning of part 2, after mentioning the words of Aristotle who believed in the existence of G-d while also believing in the eternal existence of the world, and along the same line of reasoning which Aristotle brought for the existence of G-d and that He is one and not physical. The Rambam rose to argue with him and refute his proofs on the eternity of the world, and to demonstrate that Aristotle has no proof on this, until just the opposite - one can prove the creation. However, the author here, of blessed memory, sifted the truth from the words of the philosophers, and added strength and pure hands to revive the proofs for creation and to mend their breaches, and automatically the existence of G-d will be demonstrated.

Regarding the necessity of all three premises, since the main proof stands on the "chidush haolam" (that this world was brought into existence from nothing), and from there we begin to clarify the existence of G-d, namely, from the visible to the invisible, therefore it was necessary to bring these three premises, because from the first premise alone, the non-believer can claim: "whatever created this world was itself created from another cause, and that cause also has a cause, and so on endlessly". Therefore, he added the second premise. And lest the non-believer refute saying that this world is without beginning (eternal), he added the third premise.)

The proof of these three premises is as follows.

PROOF OF FIRST PREMISE

Anything that exists, after it had not existed, cannot escape one of two possibilities: Either it created itself or something else created it.

If it created itself, then, also it cannot escape one of two possibilities: Either it created itself before it existed or after it existed.

Both are impossible, because if we suppose that it created itself after it existed, then it did nothing, since it was not necessary to make itself because it already existed before doing anything, therefore, it did nothing.

If we suppose it made itself before it existed - at that time it was *"efes v'ofes"* (absolutely nothing - TL), and that which is efes (nothing) cannot perform any action nor preparation (potential) for action, because nothingness cannot do anything. Therefore, it is impossible for something to make itself in any way.

The first premise has been clarified.

> (*Tov Halevanon commentary* on *"efes v'ofes"*: this means that which is absolutely nothing, with no potential nor any way that would leave a possibility of existence in it. He doubled the term merely to emphasize the matter.
>
> *Translator:* Modern Physicists have discovered that **transient "virtual particles"** appear and disappear in vacuum space for extremely brief time intervals (quantum fluctuations). Some prominent atheists claim this is a refutation to the premise that a thing cannot create itself and propose that it is possible for the universe to simply appear out of nothing. In the USA, The Discovery channel's first episode of the first season of Curiosity (entitled "Did God Create the Universe?" by professor Stephen Hawking) said the following:
>
>> "...you enter a world where conjuring something out of nothing is possible (at least, for a short while). That's because at this scale particles, behave according to the laws of nature we call 'quantum mechanics', and they really can appear at random, stick around for a while, and then vanish again to reappear somewhere

else."

Another example: Professor Lawrence Krauss, a high profile American theoretical physicist and cosmologist with a long list of important positions and best selling books, claims in his best selling book *A Universe from Nothing*:

> "Just the known laws of quantum mechanics and relativity can produce 400 billion galaxies each containing 100 billion stars and then beyond that it turns out when you apply quantum mechanics to gravity, space itself can arise from nothing, as can time. It seems impossible but it's completely possible..."

Answer: First of all, quantum mechanics allows, and even requires temporary violations of conservation of energy. The virtual particles are a well established and well understood consequence of quantum mechanics - not something out of nothing. They are not uncaused events in the vacuum but rather *properties* of the spacetime vacuum. The virtual particles "borrow" for a very short amount of time the ground energy that is already available from time/energy uncertainty principles and converts that to virtual particles with $E=mc2$. Neither does this even violate the conservation laws because the kinetic energy plus mass of the initial decaying particle and the final decay products is equal. To make these 'virtual particles' in the vacuum real (longer lasting than time-uncertainty permits), you have to put in energy.

Furthermore, they don't magically disappear into nothing, but rather fluctuate in and out of observable existence due to quantum mechanical uncertainty laws (without the uncertainty principle, electrons would collapse into protons thus destroying the world). In quantum mechanics there is an extremely tiny grey area of observable uncertainty. They merely fluctuate in and out of this grey area - not that they disappear and reappear from nothing. (In truth, nothing has ever been found to be lost. Even for black holes. When light falls in, the Black Hole increases in mass. When it radiates out (Hawking radiation), it decreases in mass. Everything always balances out.) Hence, the above claims are wild and misleading extrapolations.

To summarize, a spacetime vacuum governed by quantum mechanics is still something. It is not nothing. It has a curvature which varies in proportion to whatever matter and radiation is present as has been posited by Einstein's general relativity theory and confirmed by experiments. Vacuum space even has a positive mass resulting from the cosmological constant and a positive expansion rate. There can be no property associated with "nothing" for that would be a contradiction. Likewise, only a thing can have states, and only a thing can be described in terms of physical law.

The author already guarded from these types of wild claims in saying "efes v'ofes", the double language to emphasize "absolutely nothing", as the Tov Halevanon commentary pointed out. Hence, there is no way *whatsoever* to describe quantum fluctuations or the like in non-existent space-time.

This fallacy is well explained by the American philosopher Edward Feser, here's an excerpt:

> "This is, of course, a summary of the argument of Krauss's book. And the problem with it, as everybody on the planet knows except for Krauss himself and the very hackiest of his fellow New Atheist hacks, is that empty space governed by quantum mechanics (or any other laws of physics, or even just the laws of physics by themselves) is not nothing, and not even an "example" of nothing (whatever an "example of nothing" means), but something. And it remains something rather than nothing even if it is a "good first approximation" to nothing (which is what Krauss presumably meant by "good first example"). When people ask how something could arise from nothing, they don't mean "How could something arise from almost nothing?" They mean "How could something arise from nothing?" That is to say, from the absence of anything whatsoever -- including the absence of space (empty or otherwise), laws of physics, or anything else. And Krauss has absolutely nothing to say about that, despite it's being, you know, the

question he was asked, and the question he
pretended to be answering in his book."

The full version can be read online <u>here</u>.

This is sufficient grounds to dismiss the "proofs" of the
atheist professors (actually they call themselves "anti-
theists") and no further proof is necessary. Other physicists
invoke the framework of string theory which states that there
are multiple universes and that what we call matter and
energy is a product of the collision of two or more of these
universes. this leads to a new universe with its own laws of
physics. This, they propose, because the physics of our
universe break down at the time of the "Big Bang", but of
course this assumes the "multiverse" already exists and only
leads to more questions... This is similar to the eminent
<u>scientists</u> who upon realizing the enormous complexity of
even the simplest possible living organism come to the
conclusion that it could not possibly have arisen randomly.
So they propose that aliens may have planted life on earth.
Of course this just raises the question of where did those
aliens come from? (besides being more science fiction than
science)

Among other misleading claims one may come across is
something like: "we have observed matter and antimatter
collide (ex. positive charge electron with negative charge
electron), annihilating each other and disappearing into
nothing. Therefore, the opposite could also happen - that
matter and antimatter could simply pop out of nothing." The
trick in this claim is that matter and antimatter do not
magically disappear into nothing like some kind of rabbit
trick. Rather they transform into energy radiation (photons).

The bottom line is that no matter what the method of creation
of the universe, "Something" must have always existed in
some fashion. This fundamental reality is "G-d" as we will
see. The physicists deny there is a G-d, and yet they spend
their whole lives futilely trying to quantify who and what G-d
is, whether or not they realize it. No matter what space,
energy, and mass relationships are, and regardless of
whether those quantities are finite or infinite, it follows

logically that "something" must be eternal and un-caused. Scientific inquiry can take you to the border, to the edge of the physical realm. At that border, it is apparent that something lies beyond.

As we will see, that which is eternal is of a completely different "type" of existence than anything we are familiar with. It's not like it can be held in the hand or looked at under a microscope. The Eternal exists above time, and that which is above time is also above space since the two are inextricably intertwined. If so, then it must also be unchangeable at least in the way we understand change. Since change as we know it happens in spacetime. Hence that which is eternal is inherently unknowable, unreachable and unscientific. We cannot perceive it or examine it in any way and can only deduce its existence through rational investigation and through the effects it manifests in our world. i.e. the existence of our non-eternal world. And when we examine the universe and especially life forms, we come to know that the Eternal has the characteristics of wisdom and also ability. If we reflect more, we may come to see G-d's manifestation as an over-all Intelligence, an ever-present, all pervading Spirit - which creates and sustains everything and gives life to everything.

Tov Halevanon commentary on *"efes v'ofes"*: (continuation.) Some want to explain his intent in doubling the term to refer to two types of nonexistence:
(1) that which is nonexistent in actuality but has the potential for the thing, such as a seed from the fruit of a tree, which is nonexistent from being a tree but is not nonexistent in potential, since it has the potential when placed in the soil to produce a tree.
(2) that which is nonexistent in potential and in actuality, such as a rock, which will never produce a tree.
For this he added the word: "ofes", but if so, we need to complete the proof of the author, because that which he went on to say: "because nothingness cannot do anything", even though it clarifies that something which is completely nonexistent cannot do anything, but we still don't know that the "ofes", which is something which is non-existing in actual

but exists in potential cannot do anything. To clarify this, we need to bring the eighteenth introduction from the beginning of part 2 of the Moray (Rambam's Guide for the Perplexed): "anything which comes out from potential to actual must necessarily have been taken out by something else which is external to it (i.e. you cannot have something existing eternally in potential and then suddenly - "Big Bang" all by itself. Rather, there must be something external to it which took it out to actual - translator). [Proof:] because either way,(1) if the thing which took it out from potential to actual was internal to it, and also that there is nothing [external] preventing it from coming out to actual - then it would never be in a state of potential.

(*Translator*: Later on he explains that it is impossible for such a potential to not come to actual if an eternity of time passed over it since nothing is holding it back from coming to actual. Therefore, since the past extends infinitely back, (whether in time or if time is a creation then an infinite timeless eternity extending forever back), if so there is no point in the past where we can find it existing in potential, since any point you pick will always have infinite time or infinite timeless eternity forever preceding it.)

Tov Halevanon: (2) Alternatively, if the thing which took it out from potential to actual was internal to it and there is also something [external] preventing it and holding it back [from coming out to potential], there is no doubt that this external thing which is holding it back is what will bring it from potential to actual. Understand this. We will explain further later on.

(*Translator*: To summarize: "efes" - nothing, i.e. something with no potential to become anything whatsoever, namely, that which is absolutely nothing, can certainly not produce anything, as earlier. "ofes" - Not only that which is absolutely nothing, but even something which existed eternally as a potential for something - that also cannot produce anything on its own, namely, it cannot come out from potential to actual on its own, without something which is external to it taking out of its potential to its actual.)

Tov Halevanon: Now the proof of the author is established, that something cannot make itself, and even something which exists in potential needs something else to bring it out [to actual]. End of Tov Halevanon commentary.

Manoach Halevavos: That which a thing cannot make itself applies only to something created but that which is Kadmon (eternal, without beginning) and infinite, behold, in truth, it did not make itself. This is the reason why the question of "how did G-d make Himself?" is not relevant.
(Translator: Once we have established that there must be something Eternal, otherwise nothing would exist in the present, then you cannot ask "well, what created this Eternal thing?" or "who designed this Eternal thing?". Both questions are irrelevant since the Eternal by definition always existed.)

PROOF OF SECOND PREMISE - (Beginnings are limited in number)
The proof of the second premise is as follows: (commentaries to follow)
Whatever has a limit/end (i.e. is finite) must have a beginning, because it is evident that something which has no beginning (i.e. existed eternally) has no limit/end (i.e. is finite), since it is impossible for man to fathom the limits of that which is without beginning.

Therefore, that which was found to have a limit/end, we know that it must have had a first beginning which had no beginning before it, and a starting with no starting before it. And when we consider the finite character of all the beginnings found in the world, we must conclude that they had a first Beginning with no beginning before it and a first starting with no start before it, since there cannot be an infinite chain of (non-eternal) beginnings.

SECOND PROOF THAT BEGINNINGS/CAUSES MUST BE FINITE IN NUMBER
(commentaries to follow)
Furthermore, it is evident that anything which has parts must have a whole, since a whole is merely the sum of its parts. It is not conceivable for something infinite to be comprised of parts, because a part, by definition, is an amount separated from another amount, and through the part the whole is measured, as Euclides mentioned

in the fifth treatise of his book of measures.

> *Pas Lechem :* *"through the part the whole is measured"* -
> through the part, one can know the amount of the whole. For
> example, if we know that one third of an object's length is 4
> cubits, from this we know that it's whole length is 12 cubits.

If we consider in our thoughts something which is infinite in actuality,
and we take a part from it, the remainder will undoubtedly be less
than what it was before. And if the remainder is also infinite, then
one infinite will be greater than another infinite, which is impossible.

Alternatively, if the remainder (of the whole) is now finite, and we put
back the part that we took away - then the whole will be finite, but it
was originally infinite, if so the same thing is finite and infinite which
is a contradiction and impossible. And therefore, it is impossible to
take out a part from something which is infinite, since whatever is
comprised of parts is undoubtedly finite.

Now of all things (individuals) that have ever existed in the world, if
we take out a part of this total number, such as all the individual
things that came into existence from the days of Noah to the days of
Moses. The total number of individual things of this part is finite,
therefore the whole together is also finite. And since the whole of
this world is finite in the number of its individual things, it must also
be that the number of its beginnings (causes) is also finite, and
perforce this world has a first Cause which had no previous cause,
and it is necessary because of this, that the beginnings reach an
end.

> *(some commentaries on this second premise)*
>
> THE PROOF OF THE SECOND PREMISE IS AS
> FOLLOWS:
> WHATEVER HAS AN END MUST HAVE A BEGINNING,
> BECAUSE IT IS EVIDENT THAT SOMETHING WHICH HAS
> NO BEGINNING (i.e. existed eternally) HAS NO LIMIT/END
> (i.e. is infinite), SINCE IT IS IMPOSSIBLE FOR MAN TO
> FATHOM THE LIMITS OF THAT WHICH IS WITHOUT
> BEGINNING.

Manoach Halevavos: *"whatever has an end must have a
beginning"* - "end" refers to some finiteness/limit, whether
those two endpoints (beginning/end) are in time or in causes
(that it appears as the definite effect of a cause). Likewise
any physical thing has limits in 3 dimensions, namely, its
physical dimensions. If so, it is obvious that whatever has
limits must have a beginning (is not eternally existing) (more
on this in ch.7).

"something which has no beginning has no limit/end" - it it
evident and also explained in books of wisdom that any
power which is without beginning has no limit/end (i.e. is
infinite). Just like it existed forever, infinitely, eternally back,
so too it will continue infinitely, forever. This is a sound
deduction which the intellect accepts. An intelligent person
cannot claim that something without beginning is bound, and
that he can fathom its limits. This is what he meant by "since
it is impossible for man to fathom the limits of that which is
without beginning", i.e. for man's intellect to fathom it... It
must be indestructible since it has no cause and behold a
thing cannot make itself. (i.e. if a thing cannot make itself,
and it has no cause, then how can it possibly exist?
Therefore, its essence must be beyond the limits of our finite
human logic.)

Pas Lechem: Since the thing is eternal, without beginning,
therefore, its power is infinite, since whatever is finite ceases
when its finite power ceases. Therefore, it would have
already ceased if it were finite (and would never have
reached the present). Hence that which is without beginning
cannot be finite, and since it is infinite, therefore it will never
cease to exist forever, just like it did not cease eternally. And
this is the meaning of "since it is impossible for man to
grasp...", i.e. it is impossible for man's [finite] intellect and
understanding to grasp the limit of its power and to
investigate and consider how much longer it will continue to
exist and when it will cease, according to the limit of its
power - since it must be that its power is completely without
limit.

Translator's note: If you ask: "it does not consume energy for something to exist. A rock can exist forever in the past and still not be infinite in power". Answer: A rock can theoretically exist forever as a rock but at some point it must have not existed as a rock since a rock cannot make itself, therefore something else caused its existence, such as energy, and that energy also cannot make itself and so forth until you reach a totally different "kind" of existence, of infinite power, and without beginning.

Furthermore, a rock cannot really exist forever on its own power but exists through the power of a higher Force as the Manoach Halevavos commentary points out: "some claim that even though the world is created, nevertheless, it is possible that it will exist forever, and will never cease. This is incorrect since that which the world would never cease to exist forever is not "in actual", but rather "in practice" (i.e. caused by something else), and that if the will of G-d is that it continues to exist, obviously it will continue just like He created it by His will, and if His will is not for this, it is impossible for it to continue to exist by itself. See the Moray Nevuchim part 2 introductions 1,2,3 with the commentary of Rav Shem Tov for a clearer explanation of this)

Similarly, regarding the "virtual particles" mentioned earlier, even if they did appear out of "nowhere" in space (which they don't), but even if they did, it would still not necessarily prove that they are uncaused events like some scientists claim. It just means we cannot see any cause. But the cause could well be there, we just don't see it. Indeed, all the strangeness and contradictions one encounters in quantum mechanics goes away once one realizes the physical does not have any independent existence - they is a higher Force pulling the strings and keeping track of everything. To quote Max Planck, one of the most important physicists of the twentieth century:

"As a man who has devoted his whole life to the most clear headed science, to the study of matter, I can tell you as a result of my research about atoms this much: There is no matter as such. All matter originates and exists only by virtue of a force which brings the particle of an atom to vibration and holds this most minute solar system of the atom together. We must assume behind this force the existence of a conscious and intelligent mind. This mind is the matrix of all matter".

THEREFORE, THAT WHICH WAS FOUND TO HAVE A LIMIT/END, WE KNOW THAT IT MUST HAVE HAD A FIRST BEGINNING WHICH HAD NO BEGINNING BEFORE IT, AND A STARTING WITH NO STARTING BEFORE IT. AND WHEN WE CONSIDER THE FINITE CHARACTER OF ALL THE BEGINNINGS FOUND IN THE WORLD, WE MUST CONCLUDE THAT THEY HAD A FIRST BEGINNING WITH NO BEGINNING BEFORE IT AND A FIRST STARTING WITH NO START BEFORE IT, SINCE THERE CANNOT BE AN INFINITE CHAIN OF BEGINNINGS.

Tov Halevanon commentary: This means to say that anything which has a limit/end (i.e. is finite), must also have a beginning, i.e. a start [of its existence], because something which has no end [to its existence] is only that which is infinite from all perspectives (i.e. no finiteness whatsoever). This matter also applies to [finite] things which do not actually exist together simultaneously, but rather follow each other, when this one comes [to exist], the other ceases [to exist] (such as living things where offsprings outlive parents) - that it is impossible for this to go on countlessly in endless stages until one can say that they have no first beginning, because then even the thing that is here in the present would not exist, similar to the familiar saying among the philosophers: "if the first did not exist, the last (present) would not exist", which means to say, if there was not a first beginning to the thing, then it would be impossible for the thing to exist in the present also.

(Translator: This means if you have something non-eternal in the present, you cannot explain its existence by saying that it was the effect of something else non-eternal (its "cause"), and that also was the effect of something else-non eternal (its "cause"), etc. endlessly, in an infinite regress, because this is an attempt to get something from nothing.

Fallacy of Infinite Regress of Causes
Infinite regress of causes is sometimes invoked to negate the need for a first eternal cause.

So instead of saying the universe is eternal or that it was created by something eternal, we can simply say that the universe existed and evolved from one form to another, in an infinite chain of non-eternal forms. An analogy for this: if we want to explain the existence of a chicken in the present, then instead of saying the chicken lineage had a first beginning, we can simply say that there was infinite regress of chicken/egg/chicken/egg etc. infinitely back, without beginning, where the chicken/egg/etc. regress is an analogy for the various forms of the universe.

Hence there is no need for anything eternal and the universe simply existed and evolved from one form to another, in an infinite chain of non-eternal forms. This is known as infinite regress of [non-eternal] causes.

However this is logically incoherent.
If we think of causes and effects as links in a chain, then consider that every link in the chain depends on the previous link. hence, the chain as a whole depends on something which does not even exist.

As an illustration, consider a chain hanging down from above almost touching the floor.
One asks, what is the chain fastened to?
Answer: The next link.
And what is that fastened to?
Answer: The one before that.
And that one?
Answer: The next one before, and so on...

I think it can be seen evidently that it doesn't matter whether there are a million or infinite links - there is nothing to hold up the chain. Without some tangible, real support the chain cannot hold *even if it is infinitely long*.

So too here, if you don't have something eternal, then a

chain of non-eternal links will not help to explain the existence of something in the present, even if it is infinitely long.

Furthermore, the result of an infinite regress is indeterminable unless there is some eternal source. As an illustration consider a square room with mirrored walls reflecting an image of a human being in an infinite regress simulation. If there is no source, i.e. a real human being then the picture being reflected infinitely is indeterminable. Why should it be a human face, or a chicken, or whatever?

The only possible solution would be if there is no picture in the mirrors.

So too here, unless there is "something" eternal, nothing would exist in the present. **The infinite regress is just an attempt to push off the same problem indefinitely, never solving it.**

Some want to answer this problem by saying: If history goes back ad infinitum, then there are certain causal chains involving objects of a certain kind that go back ad infinitum also. Hence, we might say that the fact that the objects in this causal chain are chickens, as opposed to fish or frogs, is just the way things happen to be. Indeed, something just happening to be the case is roughly what we take to be the condition sufficient for a state of affairs to be contingent as opposed to necessary, and the fact that there are chickens is taken to be a contingent fact.

To this we reply, that it is possible to imagine in one's mind infinite reflections of chickens in the mirrors without the existence of a source, i.e. a real chicken but the power of imagination deceives. The mind can also imagine and suppose things which are impossible in actuality. In practice, you must have something real otherwise nothing will show up in the mirrors. Trying to make the problem disappear into infinity is an illusion of the imagination.

(In the above mirror analogy, we simulated the two types of "things" in existence. One, a thing which is possessed of its own intrinsic cause (not caused by something else). Two, a thing which is dependent for its existence upon extrinsic causes (other things). There is no intermediate alternative between the two types of things. In the mirror system, the reflections appearing in the mirrors are all of the second type since their existence depends on either a previous reflection or on the human being in the room. The human being in the room is the intrinsic primary cause, since his appearance does not depend on the reflections in the mirrors. From this analogy it should be evident that a system cannot be comprised of only the second type of causes, since it as a whole would be dependent on something indeterminate (and which does not even exist!). Rather, there must be some kind of source (i.e. an intrinsic cause, something real) for the reflections otherwise nothing would exist.

To Summarize: The infinite regress is fallacious reasoning. Essentially, it attempts to account for a phenomenon in terms of the very phenomenon that it is supposed to explain. This creates an endless repetitive argument that actually explains nothing. *Manoach Halevavos:* (later) Anything that we see that must be the effect of a cause and that its existence is impossible without a cause (i.e. that it is not eternal) it must be that either (1) its cause is eternal or (2) that its cause is the effect of another cause, and that one to another, and so forth until you reach a first cause which is eternal. Because if this were not so, then the whole thing would collapse. Because since we see the effect [in the present] cannot exist without a cause, how can its cause in turn possibly exist without some firm origin which everything depends on. This is just like one who ties one rope to another and another to another in order to hang a weight on its end. It cannot work unless the other end is firmly attached to a ceiling. This is self-evident.)

SECOND PROOF THAT BEGINNINGS/CAUSES ARE FINITE IN NUMBER

(*Manoach Halevavos*: This is a second proof. The first proof relied on "self-evident" truths, namely, that it is evident that there is a limit to the number of beginnings... Now he will bring a second way in the form of a logical proof which demonstrates that the universe has a finite number of beginnings.

FURTHERMORE, IT IS EVIDENT THAT ANYTHING WHICH HAS PARTS MUST HAVE A WHOLE, SINCE A WHOLE IS MERELY THE SUM OF ITS PARTS. THEREFORE, IT IS NOT POSSIBLE FOR SOMETHING INFINITE TO BE COMPRISED OF PARTS, BECAUSE A PART, BY DEFINITION, IS AN AMOUNT SEPARATED FROM ANOTHER AMOUNT (where a small part is separated from the whole - *ML*), AND THROUGH THE PART THE WHOLE IS MEASURED, AS EUCLIDES MENTIONED IN THE FIFTH TREATISE OF HIS BOOK OF MEASURES.

(*Tov Halevanon commentary*: If we have before us many things together, then the nature which each part has on its own, will also be contained in the combined whole since the whole is the sum of its parts, and through the part we measure the whole, namely how many parts are in the whole, and since each part is finite then it must be that the combined whole is also finite. This is a clear proof that it is impossible for many combined [finite] measures together to be infinite.) (Translator: i.e. you cannot have something of infinite character from infinite finites of non-infinite character (except in the imaginary world of mathematics), since infinity is not a sum of parts but rather a special "unbounded" character. this will be explained.)

IF WE CONSIDER IN OUR THOUGHTS SOMETHING WHICH IS INFINITE IN ACTUALITY, AND WE TAKE A PART FROM IT, THE REMAINDER WILL UNDOUBTEDLY BE LESS THAN WHAT IT WAS BEFORE. AND IF THE REMAINDER IS ALSO INFINITE, THEN ONE INFINITE WILL BE GREATER THAN ANOTHER INFINITE, WHICH IS IMPOSSIBLE.

(Translator: In mathematics it is possible for an infinity to be comprised of a set of units such as the infinite set of all positive integers S={1,2,3,...} You can take out/exclude a finite subset so that S'= S - {4,5,6} and S' remains an infinite set. The two infinities can even be substracted to result in a finite set, so that S - S' = {4,5,6} with cardinality of 3. Likewise one infinity can be bigger than another infinity, for example the infinite set of all rational numbers is one infinite power bigger than the infinite set of all integers since between any two integers there are infinite rational numbers.

Hence the author's statement "one infinite will be greater than another infinite, which is impossible" is incorrect. Some scientists such as Stephen Hawking have claimed to refute this statement with such mathematical proofs.

However, on closer look, the author guarded from this in saying "something which is infinite in *actuality*", which the Marpe Lenefesh commentary explains:

"This means that the thing to consider is infinite in *actuality*, but for something which is not actually infinite but just theoretically infinite, that the mind imagines something infinite - from this one cannot bring a refutation, because the power of imagination deceives, and one can picture and think in his imagination also on impossible things. The Kuzari says in treatise 5 section 18: "it is within the power of the mind to consider thousands, and thousands of thousands multiplied over endlessly, this is in potential, but for this to come to the realm of actuality - no", see there." (End of Marpe Lenefesh commentary)

Hence some things are possible in the realm of mathematics, but are nevertheless impossible in reality. This is because mathematics is pure [human] logic and logic is not truth. Logic is merely a tool which we use to investigate topics, but anything it has to say on the subject is from premisses which we supply. So what is logically possible depends on the premisses we adopt. If, for example, we start with the premise that we have an infinite set of numbers, then mathematics can take this and work with it logically, despite that the premise may be impossible in actuality.

In reality, you cannot have an infinite quantity because *infinity is not a number.* It's not like it is somewhere on the number line. When you start walking now, you will walk 1 mile, 2 miles, 3 miles, and so on further, *but you'll never reach the point that you've actually walked infinity miles.* You cannot think of infinity as the amount of a set of items. You cannot have infinity apples - in reality, that is. Therefore, you cannot think of decreasing and increasing that "amount".

Hence, **infinity is a description not a number**. Infinity describes a thing as having no end, no limit, no boundary or edge, it literally goes on forever, ad infinitum. Because infinity is not a number, large numbers are no 'nearer' to infinity than small numbers. Number 1 trillion for example is no nearer to infinity than number 1, because the two, numbers and infinity, are in no way related. *It is then impossible to approach infinity, a thing is either infinite and immeasurable, or finite and measurable, it cannot be part way towards infinity.*

Hence, if you try to treat an infinity as a set of finites and try to manipulate it like removing or adding a part from it, you will be trapped with contradictions.

Even in the world of mathematics, you can sometimes run into trouble if you treat infinity as a number.
For example consider the infinite sum: $S = 1 + 2 + 4 + 8 + 16...$
Now multiply both sides by 2 so that $2S = 2 + 4 + 8 + 16... = S-1$ (since it is equivalent to S without the 1)
Subtract both sides by S, and $S = -1$ which is an absurd conclusion indeed.

Another simpler example: infinity + 1 is still infinity since you can't make it any larger.
Therefore infinity + 1 = infinity
and we subtract infinity from both sides proving 1 = 0

Another example, consider if space were infinite. If we draw a number line and label it 0,1,2...Infinity
Drawing a line from 1 to the end = Infinity

Drawing a line from 2 to the end = Infinity
Substracting both lengths, you get 1=0, since the first line is
1 greater than the second.

Another example, consider an infinite amount of apples.
Removing an apple should not decrease the amount, since
infinity cannot be decreased. If so, I can remove many
apples and create a new infinity from the first. Then, do the
same with the second infinity and create a third infinity, and
so forth infinitely, which seems absurd.

Nevertheless even though infinity is not considered a "real"
number, it is a useful concept to help conceptualize certain
otherwise impossible mathematical operations. For example,
1 divided by 0 is technically undefined because you can't
divide something into no segments. However, this case
comes up frequently when dealing with many math forms, so
the concept of infinity is useful. As you divide 1 by smaller
and smaller numbers, the result is a larger and larger
number. Dividing 1 into any real number of segments will
yield some real amount in each segment. But you can get
zero in each segment if you have an unreal infinity of
segments. So, technically you would say that 1/0 is
undefined, but it "approaches" infinity. Returning to the above
example of apples, mathematically, you can make many
infinities out of a single infinity. Mathematically, 2 times
infinity is just infinity. All the contradictions go away once you
realize infinity is not a real number.

Hence, it is not possible to have an infinity of anything finite
in the real world. And even if we were to suppose for
argument's sake that there are in fact infinity apples in the
universe, this is not a property of the apples rather it is a
property of the single entity called "the universe" which itself
is inherently infinite; i.e. it's not that you have infinity apples
but rather you have a higher entity called the universe which
may or may not have apples. The description "infinity"
applies to the universe not to the apples. The apples' infinity
is not their own. It is granted to them by the higher non-finite
entity which has them, namely the single infinite universe
which may or may not have apples.

It comes out of this that the only place we can find an actual infinity is in the framework of existence which you exist inside of (in our case - space). If one tries to apply infinity to anything else, he will be trapped with contradictions. I think this is the author's intent in saying: "since it is impossible for man to fathom the limits of that which is without beginning". i.e. That which is without beginning (eternal) is the ultimate framework of existence - the root framework, the Framework of all frameworks. This "Framework" is also fundamentally different than other frameworks since the existence and the framework are one and the same, unlike us for example, where the existence (body) is separate from the "framework" (space) it exists inside of. Hence, the Eternal cannot be grasped in any way. It is a completely different "type" of existence than anything we are familiar with. There is an interesting analogy brought by Rabbi Nechemia Coopersmith in an article which illustrates this distinction. Here is an excerpt:

There is a scene in Kurt Vonnegut's novel, "Breakfast of Champions", The main character, Kilgore Trout, is having a drink in a bar, minding his own business. Suddenly he senses an awesome presence about to enter the bar. He breaks out into a cold sweat. Who walks in?

Kurt Vonnegut. When the author of the book steps into the novel to visit his character, Kilgore's perception of his world turns upside down. He realizes that he does not exist independently. Rather, every moment of his life requires a new stroke of the author's pen. Without the author, he ceases to exist.

He also realizes that his universe exists only in the mind of the author, and that beyond his ephemeral world there is a higher dimension -- the realm of Kurt Vonnegut - that is more real than his own. (End quote)

With this introduction we will hopefully understand the commentaries better:

Author's words: *"If we consider in our thoughts*

something which is infinite in actuality, and we take a part from it, the remainder will undoubtedly be less than what it was before. And if the remainder is also infinite, then one infinite will be greater than another infinite, which is impossible"

Marpe Lenefesh commentary: "If we were able to take out a finite part from something infinite then perforce it must be composed of two opposite characters - finite and infinite, and this is an impossibility..."

Tov Halevanon: i.e. before we took a part from it undoubtedly it was greater than it is now. And since it is now also infinite therefore it must be equal to what it was before we took out the part since anything infinite cannot be made less (i.e. X - 1 = X which is impossible for any number.)

and earlier:
Tov Halevanon: If we have before us many things together, then the nature which each part has on its own, will also be contained in the combined whole since the whole is the sum of its parts, and through the part we measure the whole, namely how many parts are in the whole, and since each part is finite then it must be that the combined whole is also finite. This is a clear proof that it is impossible for many combined [finite] measures together to be infinite. (i.e. something of infinite character cannot be comprised of infinite finites of non-infinite character, rather only something intrinsically infinite can have infinite character.)

Along the same lines, you cannot have an infinite number of finite causes. Since each causation unit is finite, namely, that it is non-eternal, therefore, it must be the effect of another causation unit. And since the second causation unit is also finite since it too is non-eternal, therefore it too must be the effect of another causation unit. For finite causation units this cannot go on and on endlessly of the same repetitive argument - because it is viewed from a primate concept of "infinity" as a sum of "infinite" "finites". Rather, there must be an eternal Entity which is *intrinsically* infinite. The Infinity of the Creator BB"H is not at all of the same "type" of the poor and primitive "infinity" of the above far-fetched causation-argument. His Infinite-true-Infinity so to speak is different in essence of all "types" of humanly-thought-of "infinites". He is The First Cause which is inherently infinite, i.e. eternal and without beginning, H-shem, blessed be He.)

ALTERNATIVELY, IF THE REMAINDER (OF THE WHOLE) IS NOW FINITE, AND WE PUT BACK THE PART THAT WE TOOK AWAY - THEN THE WHOLE WILL BE FINITE (since both are finite - *ML*), BUT IT WAS ORIGINALLY INFINITE, IF SO THE SAME THING IS FINITE AND INFINITE WHICH IS A CONTRADICTION AND IMPOSSIBLE. AND THEREFORE, IT IS IMPOSSIBLE TO TAKE OUT A PART FROM SOMETHING WHICH IS INFINITE, SINCE WHATEVER IS COMPRISED OF PARTS IS UNDOUBTEDLY FINITE.

NOW OF ALL THINGS THAT HAVE EVER EXISTED IN THE WORLD, IF WE TAKE OUT A PART OF THIS TOTAL NUMBER, SUCH AS ALL THE INDIVIDUAL THINGS THAT CAME INTO EXISTENCE (since both are finite - *ML*) FROM THE DAYS OF NOAH TO THE DAYS OF MOSHE. THE TOTAL NUMBER OF INDIVIDUAL THINGS OF THIS PART IS FINITE, THEREFORE THE WHOLE TOGETHER IS ALSO FINITE. AND SINCE THE WHOLE OF THIS WORLD IS FINITE IN THE NUMBER OF ITS INDIVIDUAL THINGS, IT MUST ALSO BE THAT THE NUMBER OF ITS BEGINNINGS (CAUSES) IS ALSO FINITE, AND PERFORCE THIS WORLD HAS A FIRST CAUSE WHICH HAD NO PREVIOUS CAUSE, AND IT IS NECESSARY BECAUSE OF THIS, THAT THE BEGINNINGS REACH AN END (to the Source of their beginning, namely, the Creator, as he will explain next chapter - *ML*).

(Translator: The Manoach Halevavos commentary writes that this last analogy is not correct for this proof. See there. He concludes that really this whole lengthy proof is not necessary, since if a thing cannot make itself, then it is obvious that there must be an Eternal Creator which created the world from nothing [since as we will see, an eternal universe is not possible]. On the other hand, the Pas Lechem commentary learns that this last analogy is going on "time". That time itself can be divided and quantified hence it cannot be infinite and eternal.

Translator: Perhaps the author's intent is to refute the views of some religions, especially eastern ones, which are of the view that the way things are is the way they've always been. What comes around goes around. Nothing ever changes - just like there are human beings now, so too there always were. Hence, by demonstrating that infinity cannot be comprised of a sum of finites, then this view is incorrect.)

some interesting points:
Manoach Halevavos commentary: One cannot refute from the years of G-d, namely that He and His years are infinite (i.e. we see that an actual infinity can be quantified and comprised of a set of units, since G-d's existence can go back infinitely in time yet every year is finite. ANSWER: no), because there (in the realm of G-d), there is no separation or division - everything is one "entity", and it is incorrect to call some of His years a "part", because they cannot be divided in actuality but rather only in thought...furthermore time does not relate to Him, and He is not subject to it, and time does not even apply to Him because time is a creation. This is well-explained in the Moray part 2 intro 15,26.

(Translator: If you ask, we see in mathematics an infinite number of points between 1 and 2 therefore it is possible for something infinite to have parts. Answer: each point is not a part since it is defined as infinitely small. So really this is circular logic. A point is just a convenient hypothetical mathematical abstraction, and since it is defined as zero width you cannot look at it as a "part".

If one also tries to refute from "space" saying: "perhaps space can stretch infinitely yet I occupy a finite space, therefore something infinite can indeed have a part". One could answer this by saying: 'I occupy a finite space' is from the human perspective - a decidely finite perspective, not from the 'infinite perspective'. Your perception of something called 'finite space' is simply because you are finite and have no other way of experiencing Space. But that has no bearing on the true nature of space.

Alternatively, space is not really infinite but is some kind of finite sphere to contain space/time, as we see from Einstein's general relativity theory that space/time can "curve". Or from black holes, that intense gravity can cause the "fabric" of space/time to go haywire. Therefore space/time is some kind of finite character "fabric" which only appears infinite because we are inside it.

If one tries to refute saying, if G-d is infinite and the universe and its parts occupies His "space", then the universe is a part of G-d, so to speak. Therefore, something infinite can have a part. Answer: As an analogy, picture in your mind an orange fruit of shiny blue color. This orange has an existence at some level in your mind through you as long as you continue picturing it in your mind. Hence, you are the source of the orange and the orange in no way takes up any of the space in your plane of existence. So too, G-d who is the Creator of all and everything exists because of Him. His "thoughts" are continuously giving existence to the universe (as brought down in the book Tanya Shaar Yichud v'Emuna ch. 7: "G-d's Thought and Knowledge of all created beings encompasses each and every creature, for this is its very life-force and that which grants it existence from absolute nothingness."). The universe can even be infinitely big and this still in no way take up any "space" in G-d's realm since His infinity is on a higher degree plane of existence.

According to this, it is theoretically possible to have more than one thing which is infinite as long as they are on different "levels" of existence. That way a lower existence infinity does not limit a higher existence infinity in any way. Hence, G-d is the highest existence since everything depends on His existence but not vice versa, therefore His infinity is an absolute infinity while any other infinity is a "relative" infinity since its existence depends on His higher existence, of this kind of absolute infinity - there can only be

One.

I asked a great Torah scholar and gifted kabalist in
Jerusalem about the infinities mentioned in this chapter and
he wrote me back that: this does not refer to what you think
or interpret infinity. It refers to that which is really truly
absolutely and ultimately infinite. In mathematics there are
different levels of mathematical infinity such as countable
infinity vs. uncountable infinity or density of the natural
rational numbers to the irrational numbers, or rational vs.
transcendental numbers. Infinites are distinguished between
themselves (in true manner/level/standards) only if the power
of one is infinitely stronger than the other one. For example,
the infinite set of all irrational numbers is one level infinitely
bigger than the set of all rational numbers (since there are
infinite irrational numbers between any two rational
numbers), and two levels bigger than the set of all integers
(since there are an infinite number of rational numbers
between any two integers). Here too there are quite a few
principal and intrinsic levels of "infinity", similar to what and
how it is described in Chassidut, such as infinite-light, infinite
(luminary), infinite all-able. These are intrinsic levels of
infinity and some are infinitely bigger (or smaller) from each
(and from this it is also in math and HKB"H is infinite infinities
"greater" than any type or level or class or magnitude of
"infinity" - so to speak). These are part of the intrinsic
meditations of the Shema and Barush-shem verses
(something which is impossible to do here and now [i.e. it
must be learned in person]) - sensing the infinitely
bigger/smaller levels of infinity - how they are in comparison
one to another - this is the practical exercise of yichuda-ila'ah
and yichuda-tata'ah and their mutual simultaneous existence
- this IS the ONLY meaning of KNOWING H-shem.

Not so clear exactly what he meant. We see from his words
though that there can be more than one thing which is truly
infinite. The explanation must be as above, that it refers to
different levels of existence which G-d created in the chain of
worlds until our finite character world. Afterwards, I asked
him whether space is finite or infinite and he said: "space is
not and cannot be infinite." I asked for an explanation and he

said: "If (physical) space would be "infinite" it will "compete" so to speak with the Infinite BB"H...The only levels which are truly infinite are the realms of HBB"H (G-d) Himself so to speak - so called "olamot-ha'ein-sof" - all the levels of Elokut (G-dliness) which are truly Infinite in some aspect - as "light" or (going higher) as "luminary" or as "ability"/"yecholet" etc. - many different levels and sublevels of distinction in G-dliness - all truly Infinite only on different levels of Infinity as we already communicated about. Of course HBB"H can do "whatever" He wishes - but here - He determined the borders of expressions of what Infinity is and what are the true Infinites that are "His" levels so to speak and what are the limited realms, realities, and worlds." (End quote)

Another time, I asked him to explain the practical exercise of yichuda-ila'ah and yichuda-tata'ah. Here is an excerpt of his reply:

> (1) in Kriat-Shma shacharit and arvit at the end of the shma verse think for some time (still with eyes closed and hand over eyes) the thought: how the entire Creation (creations worlds etc.) - all are total nothingness zero and annihilated dust in comparison to His Infinity (yichuda-ila'ah). Make this as REAL as you can while thinking very quietly and "softly" about it.
>
> (2) Then say the verse of "baruch-shem"... - at its end - think for some time more (all still in the same position) how the entire Infinity of HBB"H - the ONE you just thought of at the end of the shma - "that-one" - is now as if being entirely "squeezed" into each and every infinitely small element of Creation (yichuda-tata'ah). (This is the opposite of the first yichud - infinity of HBB"H is also [simultaneously] in each and every zero size element of Creation - even if "zero" in "size" - the biggest "topological" paradox - intrinsic part of His true infinity.)
>
> (Translator: I asked him, "how can His entire Infinity be squeezed into each and every element simultaneously? Isn't that a case of 1+1=1?" He

answered me that you cannot say "part" of G-d is in this element and another "part" is in another element ch'v, since G-d is not comprised of parts (as before, since an actual infinity is a special "infinite character", not a sum of finite character parts). Rather all of His infinity is simultaneously in each and every element no matter how small, and it's not a contradiction since infinity plus infinity equals infinity.

The main point to get out if this, I think is not that G-d is "inside" this or inside that the way we commonly understand "inside", since G-d is beyond all and transcends all (i.e. G-d is the "place" of the universe and not the opposite). He exists in a different way than we do. Rather, the main awareness to build in this meditation is that G-d is fully "with" you and has His full attention on you, despite that you and everyone else in the universe, and even the universe itself is totally insignificant relative to His infinite existence and despite that He also has His full attention on everyone else and everything else simultaneously.

(3) Then - during Tefilah (Amidah) - think the same thought in the following manner - EVERY time there is Shem-Havayah in the brachot of the Amidah except in the last signing verse of "baruch-atah"... - except in the "ending" verses - every time you run into Shem-Havayah - stop for 10 seconds and think again about the yichuda-ila'ah as at the end of the shema-verse - and every time you say the word (the one after "baruch") "atah" in the last lines/signatures/endings of the brachot of the Amidah - stop also for 10 seconds - and think the same thought of yichuda-tata'ah as at the end of the "baruch-shem" verse above... End Quote. He told me that this exercise is merely a tiny drop in the ocean and even less - since it is only a basic "first" idea. Note that the book "Tanya" seems to exhort on doing these types of meditations. See there Shaar Yichud v'Emuna chapter 7. Also worth seeing is the book Jewish Meditation by Rabbi Aryeh Kaplan page 113 for some powerful meditations in the Amida.

Keep in mind that these practices are NOT generally endorsed by most Rabbis and can make a person "strange" if he does them too much. I included it mainly due to its relevance to this gate.

Here's an interesting excerpt from Shaarei Kedusha by Rabbi Chaim Vital Part 4 which seems similar to the above:

"(R.Chaim will now quote a book:) In the book Meiras Einayim (enlightening of the eyes), parshat Ekev, on the verse 'and to cling to Him': "I, Yitzchak the small one, son of Shmuel from Ako says, that whether for special individuals (yechidim) or for the general public, that whoever wants to know the secret of the connecting of his soul on high, and the clinging of his thought to G-d on high, in order that he acquires with that constant and uninterrupted thought, the Olam Haba (World to Come), and that G-d will be with him in this world and in Olam Haba, he should picture in front of his eyes the letters of G-d's primary Name (Yud-Heh-Vav-Heh), blessed be He, as if they are written in front of him on a book in ashuris script (sefer Torah hebrew), and every letter should be large in his eyes without limit. This means that when you put the letters of the primary Name in front of your eyes, the eyes of your imagination should be on them (i.e. picture them), and the thought of your mind and your heart on the "Ein Sof" (infinite), everything simultaneously, the seeing and the thought - both of them together. And this is the secret meaning of the true clinging mentioned in the Torah "and to cling to Him" (Deut. 30:4), or "And in Him you shall cling (Deut. 10:20), or "And you who cling to G-d" (Deut. 4:4).) End Quote. Translator: Perhaps this exercise is comparable to the above, if instead of thinking of the two simultaneously, one switches back and forth between the two - not as a real meditation, but as a "light" thought whenever one's mind is free. Warning: Frequently practicing these exercises without being sufficiently spiritually ready may damage a person or make him "strange". See the book "Path of the Just"

by Rabbi Luzzato for the correct order of ascent up
the rungs of the spiritual ladder.

PROOF OF THIRD PREMISE

The demonstration of the third premise: Anything composite is
evidently composed of more than one thing, and these things which
it is composed of must precede it by nature. Likewise, whatever
assembled the compound must also precede it by nature and by
time.

> (*Tov Halevanon*: The composite thing occurs in one of two
> ways, (1) either its parts precede it also in time, such as
> water and flour, whereby the water precedes the dough in
> time, and they also precede it by nature, namely that the
> water and the flour can exist independently without the
> existence of the dough, while the existence of the dough
> cannot exist without the existence of the water and the flour.
> (2) Or, the parts do not precede the composite [in time], such
> as the composite of a living man, for example, [1] the
> physical body and [2] the "life spirit" in a man, even though
> both were created simultaneously, nevertheless they
> precede the formation of man by nature, since the formation
> of these parts does not need the existence of man but the
> existence of man needs them. Therefore the author only
> wrote that the parts precede the composite by nature, while
> the composer precedes the composite by time and by
> nature)
>
> Translator: If you ask, are elementary subatomic particles
> composite? Answer: They can be converted to radiation
> whose energy can be combined and divided, hence it is in a
> sense plural and composite. (Also, in kabala anything
> physical is viewed as a composite of physical and spiritual
> forces).
>
> In later chapters the author will demonstrate that ultimately,
> everything is inherently composite in some sense. The only
> exception is that which is Infinite in all respects.

The *kadmon* (that which always existed), is that which has no
cause, and that which has no cause has no beginning, and that
which has no beginning has no limit/end (as before). Consequently,

that which has a beginning is not *kadmon*, and anything which is not *kadmon* is *mechudash* (created, brought into existence from nothing), since there is no third term that can be between eternal and created which is neither eternal nor created. If so, anything which is composite is not eternal, and therefore must have been created. Since the third premise has been demonstrated, all three premises have been established.

Summary of the Three Premises:

First Premise - a thing cannot make itself. If there is no framework for existence, i.e. no spacetime, no laws of physics, absolutely nothing whatsoever, then a thing cannot just pop into existence.

Second Premise: You cannot have an infinite regress of non-eternal beginnings.
This means if you have something non-eternal in the present, you cannot explain its existence by saying that it was the effect of something else non-eternal (its "cause"), and that also was the effect of something else-non eternal (its "cause"), etc. endlessly, because this is an attempt to get something from nothing.

Similarly, if you have something non-eternal in the present, it can be the cause for something else which is also non-eternal, and it could be again the cause for something else which is non-eternal, but it can never be the cause for something which is eternal and it cannot last forever - such cause and effect chains will always and must reach an end to it, otherwise - it will also be an attempt to create "something" (i.e. "infinite","eternal") out of "nothing" (i.e. "finite","non-eternal").

From these 2 premises, there must be something eternal (and ONLY ONE such "thing" as we will see)

Third Premise - Anything composite cannot be eternal. Later chapters will show that everything with any kind of finiteness is inherently composite, which rules out anything physical or more than one eternal being. End of Summary.

Note: that there are ways to attack the premises found in this gate such as that the notion of time did not exist before the Big Bang and therefore, the concept of cause/effect may be obscure (we will discuss this). Philosophers even propose avoiding the problem of an infinite cause/effect regression chain using a cycle of causes, where A=>B=>C=>A, and the like, including potentially complicated networks of mutual-causation, or they propose that really an infinite regress of causes is indeed possible or even an uncaused event is possible, since the whole problem is a paradox anyways. After all, the two premises: (1) a thing cannot make itself (i.e. everything must have a cause), and (2) there cannot be an infinite regress of causes are conflicting statements. The only way to resolve the two is if there exists something Eternal. Since they prefer not to acknowledge this, therefore, they propose, that human logic itself is questionable as to its reliability due to the flaws in our assumed premises of what is logical. Hence, according to them, we cannot rule out infinite regress or uncaused events, etc. even though these things do not seem rational.

This approach is not an attempt to answer what *must be* but rather to escape into endless and inconclusive speculation as to what *might* otherwise be. Indeed, the oracle at Delphi said that Socrates was the wisest man in Athens simply because he realized that he knew nothing. For without acknowledging the inevitable (G-d) one is doomed to run around in circles exchanging one theory with giant holes for another.

Translator: Some other evidence of G-d's existence: INTELLIGENT DESIGN - Our universe seems to be extremely fine-tuned to allow for the existence of life. Furthermore, modern advances in microbiology have provided materials for a new and enormously powerful argument to design. By observing diverse life forms we can know that the Eternal Source is not some kind of natural phenomenon, but rather is an intelligent Thinker of awesome wisdom, awesome power, and awesome ability.

HASHGACHAH PRATIS (Divine providence) - Everyday
stories from life; both from the lives of others (who one
knows and trusts) and from one's own life. If a person pays
close attention to what happens around him, he cannot help
but note the Hand of G-d in so many events in our lives.
There is no need to elaborate here.

PRAYER - If a person prays to G-d regularly, he will see G-d
answer him. That does not mean that every prayer is
answered, but it does mean that if we turn to G-d regularly,
we see totally unexpected turns of events that can only be
attributed to prayer. This can be seen (sometimes even more
vividly) with regard to the prayers of others as well.
The prayer of a Tzibur (congregation) carries more weight
that that of a Yachid (individual), and its effects are equally
more evident.

PROPHECY - Even today, the power of prophecy can be
seen when pondering the Torah's promises (can a nation
exiled from its homeland and splintered into a dozen minor
ethnic groups for 2,000 years, have the ability and resolve to
return en masse to their homeland and become a universally
recognized world power?).
Perhaps closer to home, those who have had the merit and
opportunity of meeting with the Tzadikim (righteous Sages)
of the generation know that even today, we can find shadows
of "prophecy".

This category includes the infinite wisdom in the Torah, which
is evident to all who study it in depth.

*** CHAPTER 6 ***

The application of the previous premises we mentioned to demonstrate the existence of the Creator, is as follows.

When we contemplate on this world, we find it is composite and compound. There is no part of it that does not have the character of composition and coordination. For to our senses and intellect it appears like a built and furnished house, whereby all its needs are prepared. The sky above like a roof, the land below like a carpet, the stars in their array like candles. All the objects gathered in it like treasures - everything has its need (every land has things needed for the needs of the people of that land - *TL*). Man is like the master of the house who uses all that is in it. The various types of plants are prepared for his benefit; the various kinds of animals serve his use, as David said: "You have made man to have dominion over the works of Your hands; You have put all things under his feet; All sheep and oxen, and the beasts of the field; The birds of the air, and the fish of the sea, and whatsoever passes through the paths of the seas" (Ps. 8:7).

(*Kuzari* 5:10 - Even though we don't know what benefit can be derived from most of the creations, just like we don't know the purpose of all the parts of a ship and consider some unnecessary, while the maker of the ship understands them. Likewise, we would not know the purpose of many of our organs and bones if they were detached in separate pieces and placed before us, even though we use them, and it is clear to us that if one of them were missing, our actions would be lacking and we would be in need of it, so too every part of the world is known and counted by their Creator, and there is nothing to add or to diminish.

Tov Halevanon: There are no plants created for nothing. Every one is for man's need, whether for his food, his animals' food or for healing purposes [or clothing material, etc], likewise for animals, or for the benefit of their skin or for various types of healing.

Translator: If you ask - what possible benefit can there be for creatures long extinct such as the dinosaurs? Answer: the purpose of creation is human free will. Hence, it is necessary that there be room for a naturalistic explanation for everything, including life. This is why we have evidence in nature of common ancestry (evolution), or that the world appears billions of years old as a result of some cosmological accident, etc. Likewise, today we have things which don't seem to be of use to man, such as mosquitos, deep-sea creatures, or a vast universe. It's all necessary to make an environment where human free will can function. Furthermore, another purpose of nature is to teach us about G-d as mentioned in chapter 1 of Gate 2. The vast variety of creatures, teaches us about His vast wisdom. The vastness of the universe teaches us about His almighty power, how He moves these huges galaxies, etc. Hopefully with these lessons, man will learn to feel humble..

And the order of the sunrise and sunset - to establish the daytime and nighttime, and the rising and lowering of the sun to establish the heat and the cold, the summer and the winter, for the matters of the seasons and their benefits, and their continuous changing according to this order without interruption as written "Who commands the sun, and it rises not; and seals up the stars." (Iyov 9:7), and "You make darkness, and it is night" (Ps. 104:20).

And the orbits of the planets, with their various movements and periods, and the stars and constellations who follow precise movements and exact order, without straying and without changing, and the purpose of everything is for the benefit of mankind, as Solomon said: "To every thing there is a season, and a time to every purpose under the heaven" (Eccles. 3:11), and "also He has set the world in men's hearts" (Eccles. 3:1).

And everything, whether in part or as a whole, can be observed to be composite and compound. When we examine a plant or a live creature, we find them composed of the four elements - fire, air, water, and earth, which are separate and different.

(*Tov Halevanon* - This we can observe after burning something, the fire can be seen, the air which is the smoke rises, the moisture in the smoke is the element of water, and the ashes are the element of earth)

Excerpt from Morey Nevuchim 3:14 (Rambam's Guide for

the Perplexed): "Do not ask me to reconcile all matters of astronomy that they (the Sages) stated about astronomy with the actual reality, for the science of those days was deficient, and they did not speak out of traditions from the prophets regarding these matters. Rather, because they were the wise of that period in these matters or because they heard them from the wise of that period." i.e. the Rambam is telling you not to try to reconcile his approaches with our conventional scientific understanding. Like the Sages, he was basing his teachings on the knowledge of the philospophers and mathematicians of the time period in question. (from: judaism.stackexchange.com/questions/29886)

Also, Rabbi Avraham Kook notes (regarding evolution and the age of the universe) that some scientific ideas are intentionally kept hidden, as the world may not be ready for them, either psychologically or morally:
"G-d limits revelations, even from the most brilliant and holiest prophets, according to the ability of that generation to absorb the information. For every idea and concept, there is significance to the hour of its disclosure. For example, if knowledge of the rotation of the Earth on its axis and around the sun had been revealed to primitive man, his courage and initiative may have been severely retarded by fear of falling. Why attempt to build tall buildings on top of an immense ball turning and whizzing through space at high velocity? Only after a certain intellectual maturity, and scientific understanding about gravity and other compensating forces, was humanity ready for this knowledge." from: ravkookTorah.org/NOAH60.htm

(*Translator's note*: (Note that our "fire" is not the same as the element of fire as will be explained.) In Midrashic literature, the world is viewed as being constructed of four basic elements: earth, water, air and fire (Bamidbar Raba end of 14:12; Zohar 1:27a, 2:23b-24b; Tikunei Zohar intro; Sefer Yetzirah Ch. 3; Ramban Bereishit 1:1; Etz Chaim kitzur aby'a ch.10 and many others). Some mistakenly attribute this system to Aristotle, but we know this is incorrect since they are mentioned in the Sefer Yetzira which is attributed to Abraham who lived well before him. The Sefer Yetzira was

reportedly used by master Kabalists to create life forms.
According to the Talmud (sanhedrin 65b,67b), the Rabbis of
the Talmudic era used its system to miraculously create a
calf every friday and eat it on the Sabbath (sanhedrin
65b,67b). Mystics assert that the Biblical patriarch Abraham
used the same method to create the calf prepared for the
three angels who foretold Sarah's pregnancy in the Biblical
account at Genesis 18:7 (Chesed L'Avraham Mein
Chamishi). All the miraculous creations attributed to other
rabbis of the Talmudic era are ascribed by Rabbinic
commentators to the use of this book.

The earth, water, air, fire, system is aligned with and
incorporates the physical as well as the spiritual roots of this
world, while modern science's system, which combines
everything with E=mc2 describes only the physical side of
reality. This is good for engineering purposes but it is merely
the tail of the elephant of what constitutes reality.

The spiritual side of reality cannot be detected by physical
instruments. This is because they are driven not by physical
forces but by spiritual forces, namely, virtue and morality or
their opposite, both of which have no place in the scientific
paradigm. In many places throughout the book, the author
hints at these forces such as in Gate #8: "And when you do
this with a faithful heart and a pure soul, your mind will
become illuminated... A new, strange, supernal sense will
arouse in you, unfamiliar to you of all the senses you are
used to knowing..". I have personally met some rare
individuals in Jerusalem with varying degrees of such "sixth
sense", best not to elaborate... Generally, these people shun
publicity at all cost and certainly never advertise. Those who
"advertise" are always charlatans or worse. For the skeptics
out there, I refer you to the words of the famous Kabalist
Rabbi Yaakov Hillel, who is considered the expert on the
subject in the Jewish world. He even wrote a book against
such things called "Faith and Folly". Nevertheless, even he
concedes that such things do exist. Here is an excerpt of his
words from an audio lecture he gave:
http://audio.ohr.edu/track/id=521
(at 46:01) "sometimes some of these people seem to have

some sort of power of intuition. they can be quite prophetic. impressively. they can know hidden things. sometimes I've checked it out and I found out they have a well organized system of obtaining information (i.e. they are charlatans) ... but others really have this type of power... (skipping to 51:18) we should not be impressed when we see someone who knows hidden things...there are these types of things. It exists. but that's not what impresses us."

In the purely physical plane (the realm of science), the four elements parallel the <u>four primary states</u> of matter - solid, liquid, gas, plasma (some say energy). Further still, they parallel <u>the four dimensions</u> of space-time (space=3+time=1), <u>four fundamental forces</u> in physics (gravitational, electromagnetical, strong nuclear, weak nuclear), four main particles (proton, neutron, electron, photon, all governed by the <u>four fundamental mathematical operations</u> +-x/).

Interestingly, Dr. Michael Denton points out in his excellent book "Nature's Destiny" several examples of the number four appearing throughout molecular biology. In page 192 there he writes: "we have also seen that because of the natural twist in the DNA double helix, protein recognition motifs such as the alpha helix can only feel about 4 bases in the DNA double helix. It has often been said that G-d is a mathematician; on the evidence of molecular biology we might add that He is keen on the number four".

Likewise, in the life plane, they parallel the four types of life forms - inanimate (earth), plant (water), animal (air), human (fire). For in truth, the underlying reality is not atoms and subatomic particles as scientists believe, but rather - life. Life is the underlying reality. It is manifest to different degrees in this world, namely, the four degrees mentioned above. The lowest being inanimate objects where it is concealed to the utmost degree. As we go up to plants, the hand of G-d begins to be noticeable as the machine analogy breaks down. Something else is manifest there beyond the molecules. It grows and builds itself autonomously. Order seems to prevail over disorder. There is a creative Power manifest. Further up, we find consciousness in animals, a higher form of life and further still free will and morality in humans. In all these things, the machine analogy breaks down... G-d is life in its most true form, most real form - eternal life. He is the source of all life.

In the human lower soul, they parallel the four traits which must be rectified before connection with higher spiritual forces is possible - sadness (earth), lust for indulgence (water), useless speech (air), arrogance/anger (fire). Ascending higher to the higher soul, they represent the four levels of soul - nefesh (earth), ruach (water), neshama (air), chaya (fire). These are rooted in the four spiritual worlds which in turn are rooted in the four levels of Torah interpretation and ultimately in the four letter Tetragramaton Name of G-d, who continuously gives life and sustains all of creation. (see the book Shaarei Kedusha for more details).

THE MYSTICAL FIRE
Translator: In truth, the fire that we know is not the element of fire in its pure form. The only place where this special, elemental fire manifested in the physical universe was on the altar of the first temple in Jerusalem, as the Maharsha comments on Yoma 21b "because it (the fire on the altar) was the elemental fire, unlike our fire which is a composite of other elements, hence it can be extinguished by the other elements, such as water. This is what the Talmud means "the fire of the altar was never extinguished by rain", this is because there was mixed with it, the higher form of fire, the elemental fire. And that which the Torah says (Lev. 6:6) "Fire shall be kept burning upon the altar continually; it shall not go out" (which implies that it is possible to extinguish) - This refers to the second kind of fire, namely "our fire" which the Kohen brought wood, since it was a commandment to bring fire from below." End quote. Hence, the fire on the altar contained both types of fire. One, our fire which the Kohen kindled with wood and two, a higher form of fire, the elemental fire. The elemental fire cannot be extinguished through "physical" water. Hence, despite that the altar was outdoors and exposed to rain, snow, and the strongest winds of the Jerusalem winter, the weather was incapable of

extinguishing the fire on the altar.

The Talmud says there (Yoma 21b) that this kind of fire did not produce smoke, and it consumed water just like it consumed dry things. The fire consumed at a supernatural speed thousands of sacrifices each day, since behold, King Salomon alone brought 1000 burnt offerings every day despite that the area of the fire was only a few square meters and despite that only two logs of wood were added to the daily arrangement each day (Yoma 39a). Hence, it consumed the flesh and bones of entire animals at a miraculous rate.

The Talmud in (Yoma 21b) discusses the different types of fire:

> The Master said: 'And the [smoke arising from the] pile of wood on the altar'. [Question] But was there smoke arising from the pile of wood? Has it not been taught: Five things were reported about the fire of the pile of wood: It was lying like a lion, it was bright like the sun, its flame was of solid substance, it devoured wet things like dry things, and it caused no smoke to arise from it? [Answer] What we said [about the smoke] referred to the wood from outside [i.e. our type of wood-kindled fire mixed inside]. For it has been taught: And the sons of Aaron the priest shall put fire upon the altar - although the fire comes down from heaven, it is a mitzva to bring fire from outside too.
>
> 'Lying like a lion'. But has it not been taught: R. Hanina, deputy high priest, said: I myself have seen it and it was lying like a dog? - This is no contradiction: The first statement refers to the first Temple, the second to the second Temple. But was the fire present at the second Temple? - Surely R. Samuel b. Inia said: What is the meaning of the scriptural verse: And I will take pleasure in it [we-ikabed] and I will be glorified? The traditional reading is 'we-ikabedah', then why is the [letter] 'he' omitted [in the text]? To indicate that in five things the first Temple differed from the second: in the ark, the ark-cover, the

Cherubim, the fire, the Shechinah, the Holy Spirit [of Prophecy], and the Urim-we-Thummim [the Oracle Plate]? - I will tell you, They were present, but they were not as helpful [as before, i.e. the fire consumed at a much slower rate].

Our Rabbis taught: There are six different kinds of fire: (1) Fire which consumes but does not drink; (2) fire which drinks but does not eat; (3) fire which consumes and drinks; (4) fire which consumes dry matter as well as wet matter (water); (5) fire which pushes fire away; (6) fire which consumes fire.
(1) 'Fire which consumes but does not drink': that is our fire [since water extinguishes it];
(2) 'which drinks but does not eat': the fever of the sick;
(3) 'consumes and drinks': that of Elijah, for it is written: And it consumed up the water that was in the trench;
(4) 'consumes dry as well as wet matter': the fire of the pile of wood [on the altar of the temple];
(5) 'fire which pushes other fire away': that of Gabriel (the Midrash explains that when Abraham was hurled in a fiery furnace, the angel Gabriel came, whereby the fire was repelled out of the furnace and burned everyone in its outside vicinity);
(6) 'fire which consumes fire': that of the Shechinah (divine presence), for a Master said: He put forth His finger among them and burned them (the angels, which are made of a kind of spiritual fire, who advised against creating man). [It is stated above], 'But the smoke arising from the pile of wood, even all the winds of the world could not move it from its place'.

Some other sources on this subject:
Ramchal - *Mevo L'Sefer Haklalim*:

The philosophers and scientists can grasp only the external surface of the world, namely, the physical world, according to what appears to their physical eyes. However, this is merely the outermost garment of the spiritual roots, namely, the sefiros who govern the world and are the innermost spirituality inside the physical... Just like the form of man alludes to the entire system of Divine governance, so too it is alluded from all the parts of nature, and every creation is an expression of one detail of His governance...

And on this are based most of the sayings of the Sages which refer to the Creation and to all matters of the world, whether in heaven or on earth and all of their derivatives, this is also a broad and important subject.

When our Sages instruct us on matters of nature and of this world, they are referring to its inner aspect - not on its external garment. Therefore, sometimes in their words we find things which appear strange, and which appear to be clearly false from what we perceive with our senses. But the truth is that they are speaking according to the true governance which is hidden from human eyes, which they received from the prophets and from the holy Torah...

Sefer HaBris *(Maamar 5 ch.3)*

"the early philosophers agreed with the view of the Kabalists regarding the four elements fire, wind, water, earth..... The later philosophers then rose up to completely destroy the view of the early philosophers and denied it saying it is not so. This is their way, one builds and another destroys, one dreams and another interprets... Some completely denied the matter of physical and form, and slashed mercilessly, others denied the four elements, others still held there are 3 elements... either way all of the later philosophers held there is no element of fire... and after time, they agreed that there is fire in the depths of the earth...and this view is supported by the volcanos in Italy and other places.... The bottom line is that all of their views are completely unreliable... and we have already received a tradition that there indeed exists four elements fire, wind, air, water like the view of the ancient ones, and that they are joined from physical

and form, because thus wrote the man of G-d, Rabbi
Chaim Vital zt'l in Etz Chaim (shaar kitzur aby'a
ch.10), and his words are living, enduring, and faithful
forever and ever.

If you ask: "if this four element system is superior why were
the ancients so ignorant technology wise. Modern science
has brought us far superior advances in medicine, and
technology etc.?" The answer seems to be that G-d withheld
the discovery of technology for so long to protect man from
destroying himself, like a child who is given a toy plastic
hammer instead of a real metal hammer so that he won't hurt
himself. Man is much too dangerous to be given access to
nuclear weapons. Technology may seem good to us now, but
after 50 or 100 years we may look back and see that it was
not a good thing - it can really bring TREMENDOUS
destruction. As to why G-d allowed it in our times, this is
because we are near the end of days, as we can see the
prophecies of the end of days being fulfilled before our eyes
as the Jewish people return to their homeland and many
other signs. The Zohar (commenting on Bereshit 7:11)
actually predicted that technological advancement will start in
the year 5600, as a precursor and preparation for the
Messianic Era (read about it here dafyomireview.com/430).
However, all this requires many introductions to explain
properly.. Another possible explanation as to why technology
was withheld is that it is necessary to maintain free will.
Advances in microbiology are increasingly unraveling the
inner workings of cells and this is leading to a new and
enormously powerful argument to design. Scientists are
backing themselves further and further into a corner for the
more wisdom they discover, the harder it becomes to
attribute it all to chance, and to unguided natural processes.
Perhaps this is the intent of the Zohar's prediction.

(back to the book)
We do not have the capability to join the four elements, in the
natural way we find them compounded in nature because they are
different and even repel each other. If we attempt to artificially
combine them, the result rapidly changes and disintegrates, while
the synthesis brought about through nature is complete and

endures until the (appointed) time of its end.

Some of the philosophers thought that the planets, stars, supernal Ishim (type of spiritual beings - *PL*) are from the element of fire (this was the accepted scientific view among most in his time - *TL*), and similar to this David said: "Who makes winds His messengers; Flames of fire His ministers" (Ps. 104:4), and this is a support for this view, and that they are not of a fifth element (quintessence) as Aristotle held.

> (And since there is a proof from reason and scripture that they are from the element of fire, it is no longer necessary to bring a proof that they are not eternal - *TL*)

Since all existing things that we find are from the elements, and composed of them, and we know that they were not combined on their own, and by their inherent nature do not join together because of their repelling characteristics, it is clear to us that something else must have joined them and bound them, and fused them together against their nature, by force - this is their Creator, who joined them and ordained their union.

If we investigate the four elements, we will find them to be composed of Matter *(chomer)* and Form *(tzura)* which are the Essence *(etzem)* and Incident *(mikre)*.

> (*Marpe Lenefesh*: There was already much discussion from the early Sages, the philosophers, and receivers of the true tradition on the subject of "physical and form", as you can see in the Moray, the Kuzari book, the Raavad's introduction to the book of Yetzira, and the Ramban's commentary on the verse: "And the earth was without form, and void" (Gen. 1:2), see them. The summary of what comes out of all of them is as follows: When G-d wished to create the world, He first created a primordial physical without form (energy?), similar to clay in the hands of a potter, or raw metal which the metal smith uses to make various objects of different forms, but of the same material. So too regarding the four elements, before each one received the form visible to us, it was first composed of the primordial substance, which is called by the Greeks, "hiyuli", and in the kabalistic books, "nefesh yesodot", since the form requires the underlying physical,

without which it cannot hold its form, and the substance is the essence of the thing while the form is the incident *(mikre)*, because sometimes it is embodied in this form and sometimes in another. The physical and the form of the four elements always existed simultaneously, because their existence preceded that of all the creations, and from them all creations were composed...now you will understand well the author's coming words)

The [formless] Matter of the elements is the primordial matter, which is the root of the four elements, the physical or "hiyuli" of them.

(For other creations, their physical is a combination of the four elements, but the physical of the four elements is the primordial physical which has no underlying physical before it, it is the root of the four elements, and it is simple, not composite - *PL*)

Translator: Ultimately, later on we will see that everything is in some sense composite (except the underlying essence of all - G-d)

Their Form is the primordial form which comprises all forms, and which is the root of all forms, whether essence or incident such as heat (which is essence in fire but incident in other things - *ML*), cold, wetness, dryness, heaviness, lightness, movement, rest, etc.

[To summarize], combination and union are apparent throughout the world, as a whole and in all of its parts, in its roots and in its branches, in that which is simple (i.e. even in the four elements which are a union of only two things, namely the primordial matter and the Form - *ML*) and in that which is complex, in that which is above and in that which is below. Therefore, based on our previous premises, it follows that the world is entirely *mechudash* (created), since it has been clarified that whatever is composite must have been brought into existence. Therefore it is proper for us to conclude that the world is *mechudash*, and since this is so, and that it is not possible for something to make itself, therefore it must be that there was a Maker who started it and brought it into existence.

(*Marpe Lenefesh*: And even the supernal realms (angels, mystical worlds) are also composite from the four spiritual elements. They are composed from the four letters of the tetragrammaton (YHVH, G-d's primary Name as He manifests Himself to His creations), which is the source of the four spiritual and the four physical elements, and there is nothing whether in the upper realms or in our world which is not composed from the four letters of the tetragrammaton, and the Ein Sof ("light" of G-d) which dons them, as written in Shaarei Kedusha part 3 gate 1, and the Alshich on parsha Bereishis, see there)

And because we have demonstrated that it is not possible for there to be an infinite chain of causes, it must be that there was a first Cause without a previous cause and a Beginning without a previous beginning - and He is the one who formed it and brought it into existence from nothing, not with the help of anything nor for anything.

(*Marpe Lenefesh*: that there was nothing forcing Him to create the world, neither was it for His benefit, but rather, He created everything to bestow good to another, like the nature of the good to bestow good. For, we saw that of everything He created, it is only that which is needed for man and not more. While according to G-d's infinite power and ability, this entire world is as nothing. For He bestows good on everything according to what it is capable of receiving)

As the verse says on this matter: "I am the L-ord that makes all things; that stretches forth the heavens alone; that spreads abroad the earth by Myself" (Isaiah 44:24), and "He stretches out the north over the empty place, and suspends the earth over nothing" (Iyov 26:7). He is the Creator, Whom we have investigated and sought with our reasoning and intellect. He is the *Kadmon* (Eternal) which there is no beginning to His beginning, and the First, whose eternity is endless, as written: "I am first and I am last" (Isaiah 44:6), and "Who has performed and done it, calling the generations from the beginning? I the L-ord, the first, and with the last, I am He" (Isaiah 41:4).

There are some people who claim that the world came into being by chance, without a Creator who created it and without a Maker who formed it. It is amazing to me how a rational, healthy human being could entertain such a notion. If such a person heard someone else saying the same thing about a water wheel, which turns to irrigate part of a field or a garden, saying that it came to be without a craftsman who designed it and toiled to assemble it and placed each part for a useful purpose - the hearer would be greatly amazed on him, consider him a complete fool, and be swift to call him a liar and reject his words. And since he would reject such a notion for a mere simple, insignificant water wheel, which requires but little ingenuity and which rectifies but a small portion of the earth - how could he permit himself to entertain such a notion for the entire universe which encompasses the earth and everything in it, and which exhibits a wisdom that no rational human intellect is capable of fathoming, and which is prepared for the benefit of the whole earth and everything on it. How could one claim that it came to be without purposeful intent and thought of a capable wise Being?

It is evident to us that for things which come about without the intent of an intender (i.e. an intelligence) - none of them will display any trace of wisdom or ability. Behold and see, that if a man suddenly pours ink on clean paper, it would be impossible for there to be drawn on it orderly writing and legible lines like it would be with a pen, and if a man brought before us orderly writing from what cannot be written without use of a pen, and he would say that ink was spilled on paper, and the form of the writing happened on its own, we would be quick to call him a liar to his face. For we would feel certain that it could not have happened without an intelligent person's intent.

Since this appears impossible to our eyes for mere symbols (the alphabet) whose form is merely conventional, how could one entertain the notion for something whose engineering is far more fine, and whose formation is infinitely more fine, deep and beyond our comprehension, to say that it is without intent of an Intender, and without the wisdom of a wise and powerful Being.

What we have brought to establish the existence of the Creator from the aspect of His deeds should be enough for anyone who is intelligent and admits the truth, and it is a sufficient refutation to the group of kadmut, who claim the world is *kadmon* (always existed), and to disprove their claims. Know it well!

Translator: - If you ask, if so what brought G-d into existence? Why is He the exception to this rule? Answer:

G-d is eternal. You cannot ask what brought the eternal into existence. All these author things cannot be eternal as the author will explain the things which disqualify something from being possibly eternal. This will leave out everything except the true Unity.

If you ask, "hasn't Darwin's theory of evolution refuted the argument by design?" Answer: not in the least. If you look closely at the evidence, you will see that none of them ever address this point. Everything they bring is for side issues, such as proving common ancestry through DNA similarities or the like and then extrapolating to this point. But as for random processes making new engineering of non-trivial complexity - there is always a trick to their words. If you can't see the trick in an example they bring or theorize, email me and I'll show you.

(Final words from *Marpe Lenefesh* commentary: In the Moreh Nevuchim (Rambam's Guide for the Perplexed) Chapter 13: "I say that any work done with intent must have a purpose for which it was done... and likewise it is clear that the thing which was made with intent is *mechudash* (created) after there was not... And Aristotle already clarified that the plants were created for the creatures, and likewise for other things, each one for the other, and all the more so for the limbs of the creatures. Know that this existence of plan and purpose in natural matters brought the philosophers to believe in a beginning beyond nature... Know that the greatest proof to the chidush of the world, for one who admits the truth, is from the natural world around us, since all of them have a purpose and that each one is for the other - this is a proof on intent from an Intender, and intent which is carried out..." End of the Rambam's words.

I wrote this because even though the Rambam greatly engaged in debating and refuting all the different viewpoints, whether for *kadmon* (eternal existence of the world) whether for creation, as you can see in that entire book, this is what he found most proper in his eyes from all the proofs, and he brought it as his final words. In truth, it is a foundation and root. Therefore, the author (of this book) also built all of his building on it, since they are things which can be [tangibly] grasped intellectually - but to delve deeper in these matters is extremely dangerous, as the Rambam wrote in the Moreh part 2 chapter 16: "When it became clear to me [that arguments can be made against each of the proofs that Aristotle brought to show that the world was eternal (and not created), and therefore] the question of whether the world is kadmon (eternally extant) or created remains unresolved [through philosophical proofs], I chose to resolve the question based on the prophecy of the prophets, since prophecy is able to clarify matters that are beyond the power of the intellect to resolve and even those who believe that the world is eternal do not deny the existence of prophecy....", see there.

And in part 2 chapter 17, he brought a very powerful analogy against the heretics who believe in kadmut (eternal existence of the world), and he said that all of their proofs and logic are only from the nature which exists in the world after the Creator has already created them in perfect form from all angles as they are now. But how can we possibly bring a proof from this as to how it was before it was created and called to existence from nothing: "the analogy of this is to a child who was born in a deserted island, and then his mother died, and this orphan never saw a female. When he grew up and matured intellectually, he asked his father how a man was formed. His father answered him 'each person among us, came to be and was formed in the belly of a female, who is of our kind, like us, of such and such form, and the man was in her belly, small, and his body was closed. And he grew there slowly, slowly, for fixed months until the time he was forced to go out from her belly through an opening which opened for him. Afterwards he grew until he became mature in his limbs, senses, and intellect, as you see now.'

The orphan started to deny all of this, and built proofs against all these true things, saying that "they are impossible and are lies, because how is it conceivable that a live man can breathe through his nostrils inside a container which is closed on all sides, and it appears impossible that one can live for any time without breathing, or if one cannot excrete the waste of his food, he will die a painful death, and how could his mouth be shut and his navel open, and his eyes closed and his limbs constricted together for such a long time, and when he comes out of there, all of his limbs and his eyes should be intact". This is a clear proof that the formation of man could not have occurred in this way, even though it is truly so.

He ends off: "contemplate this analogy and test it, and you will find the two matters to be identical, and that we are of these who pursue Moshe Rabeinu, peace be unto him, and Avraham our forefather. We believe the world came to be in such and such a way, and it was such and such, and it was created such and such, and afterwards Aristotle came to refute our words, and he brought proofs from the laws of this nature, which are complete and with us, here in the present, but which are not comparable to what existed at the time of creation, for this was after absolute non-existence..."

He then finishes: "and you must be careful in this matter as it is a great protective wall, which I have built around the Torah.. to protect from the stones of all who hurl at it", until here is the Rambam, see also what is written in the introduction of the book "Haemunot". Note it well!)

(*Translator:* Rabbi Dovid Gotlieb has a nice lecture on the Rambam's analogy. see www.audio.ohr.edu/track/id=2006)

*** CHAPTER 7 ***

The demonstration of the Creator is one is as follows. Since it has been clarified to us, through logical proofs, that the world has a Creator, it is incumbent on us to investigate on Him, whether He is one or more than one and we will demonstrate the truth of His unity from seven arguments.

FIRST ARGUMENT FOR THE UNITY OF G-D

The first, from our examination of the causes of existent things. When we investigate on them, we find that causes are always fewer than their effects, namely, the higher up one ascends into the chain of causes, the fewer the number of causes, and the more and more one ascends this chain, the fewer and fewer will be their number until eventually one reaches one Cause, which is the Cause of all causes.

The fuller explanation of this: Individual things (Ishim) that exist are countless. When we investigate the kinds (minim), which comprise them, we will find their number to be fewer than the individuals under them, because each kind includes many individuals, and they are not countless. And when we categorize the kinds into (broader category) "types" (sugim) which includes the kinds, we will find the number of types to be fewer than the number of kinds, since each type includes many kinds, and the more one ascends the fewer the number, until one reaches the primary types.

> (Translator: The commentaries will now bring a lot of background information which will be useful throughout.)
>
> (*Tov Halevanon:* Every thing and every creature by itself is called an "individual" (Ish), such as one man or one living thing like a horse or mule or a grass or a tree. The term "kind" (min) refers to a group of individuals such as the species of man or the species of horses. The term "group" (geder) refers to something which includes many "kinds" such as "living creature", which includes the species of man and all the various living things (animals, birds, fish, etc). The term "type" (sug) is more general, as you would say the term "growing (thing)" includes all the trees and plants and all the living creatures. There is a higher "type", namely "composite"

(murkav of the elements) which includes inanimate objects like stones, metals, and all growing (living things). There is another type even more inclusive, such as the term "physical" (geshem), which also includes the four elements, but which only includes physical things, until the term "essence" (etzem), which includes every existing thing, whether physical or spiritual. This is the type which is over and above (most general) and is called the supernal type.

Pas Lechem: If I were to properly explain the following matter, our discussion would become very lengthy. One who wishes to know should get a hold of the book "Ruach Chen" and the book "Milot Higayon"; there he can quench his thirst.

Tov Halevanon: The intent of the author is to ascend to the first cause, therefore I did not need to explain here the matters of Mikre (incident).

The philosopher (Aristotle) already said that the general types are ten: Etzem, Kama, Eich, Mitztaref, Ana, Matay, Matzav, Kinyan, Poel, and Nifal. (explanation in below commentaries)

MIKRE (incidental/accidental properties) VS. ETZEM (essence)
Pas Lechem: In order to understand the following things, you need to know that all the philosophers agreed that everything that exists in the world is composed of Etzem (essence) and Mikre (incident). The Etzem is the essence of the thing, which never changes as long as the thing exists, through it we are able to know what it is and what is its essence.

Tov Halevanon: (from beginning of Chapter 8) Mikre is something which is not essential for the thing and it can exist without it, sometimes it is attached to it and sometimes not, while something which is in its essence is found on it always.
Translator: For example, hotness is something found in hot water as Mikre (incidental property), but in fire it is essence, since you can remove the hotness from water without destroying the water but you cannot remove the hotness from fire without destroying the fire.

(*Pas Lechem:*

The Mikre (incident) is that which could happen or occur to the Etzem (essence), sometimes like this and sometimes like that. The Etzem is always one thing while the Mikre divides into nine parts through which all things are included. They are upper types... Rabbi Yaakov the son of the Chacham Tzvi wrote that they correspond to the "ten sayings" (through which the world was created as brought in Pirkei Avot) and the "ten sefirot" (in kabala), and he explained them there one by one, examine there (Lechem Shamayim Ch.2 Chagiga). Perhaps they (the gentile philosophers) found them from an early book of one of our Sages, and stole and denied and put it in their bags as they did for other wisdoms they ruled over and called it on their names, as written in the Kuzari book (maamar sheni ot 1).

(THE 9 ATTRIBUTES OF MIKRE (incidental properties, non-essence)

Kama: This is when you describe a thing by its measure, namely, when you wish to label it by its measure and you call it "the long" or "the short", "the tall" or the "low height". This is an internal measure. An external measure is for example when you say "the one" or "the two", or "the three".
Eich: This is when you describe and label something by one of its physical or nonphysical properties, for example, you describe it "the white" or "the black", or "the solid" or "the liquid". (not sure what he means by nonphysical - translator).
Mitztaref: When you describe this thing and label it relative to something else and through this label, both are described, such as when you describe this one as a "father" or a "master". From this label we know for certain that he has a son or a servant, since there is no father without a son and no master without a servant..
Ana: This is when you describe something and give a sign by its place. For example: Mr. X who lives in house Y or in city Z.
Matay: Describing and labeling a thing by a known time, for example, Mr. X born at date and time Y.
Matzav: Describing something through its situation, for example "the sitting" or "the lying down" or "falling on his face".

Kinyan: Describing a thing by the possessions it acquired for itself, for example "he is wearing X clothing" or "with hair X", as long as it is not separated from it, it can be described through this.

Poel and Nifal: All the books have these two in reverse order.. this refers to describing the Etzem (essence) by one of the changes in it, or that it divests itself of one form and dons another, such as earth which changed to a mouse (through food, etc ingested by its mother), or through an incident that it's measure changes, that it was small and grew, or that it was white and darkened.

Nifal: That you describe the "doer" through changes which occurred to the thing "done unto". Because everything "done unto" has an external "doer" which causes it these changes. For example, that you say that from the tree was "done" a chair, the changes to the etzem of the tree happened indirectly and the craftsman who caused the changes is the one who did them. Likewise for something which existed in potential and went out to actual, and changed from potential to actual - there must have been an external "doer" which brought out this potential to actual.

For the rest of their details, divisions, and explanations, see the Moreh and the "Ruach Chen" chapter 10, and the other books dealing with them. The summary of all of them is what I wrote, and this is enough to understand the author's words)

The causes of these ten general types are five: Motion and the four elements - Fire, Air, Water, and Earth. (since without motion nothing can come to be or change - *PL*).

The causes of the four elements are found to be two: Matter (chomer) and Form (tzura), and if we further examine on the cause of these two, undoubtedly it will be less than them. This (cause) is the will of the Creator, and there is no number less than two but one, if so, the Creator is one.

And likewise David, peace be unto him, said: "Yours, O L-ord, is the kingdom and You are exalted as head over all" (Chronicles 29:11), which means that G-d is exalted above all that is exalted, lofty above all that is lofty. He is the First of all beginnings and the Cause of all causes.

THE SECOND ARGUMENT FOR THE UNITY OF G-D

The second argument is drawn from the perspective of the signs of wisdom manifested in the universe, whether above or below, in the inanimate, plants, and animals on it.

When we contemplate the world, it will become apparent that - it is the design of one Thinker, and the work of one Creator. We find its roots and foundations to be similar in its derivatives and uniform in its parts. The signs of wisdom manifested in the smallest of the creatures as well as the biggest testify that they are the work of one wise Creator. If this world had more than one Creator, the form of wisdom would exhibit different forms in the different parts of the world, and vary in its general character and divisions.

> *Pas Lechem :* Even though the creatures are different in size, they are very similar in the amount of the Creator's wisdom exhibited by them. Just like the elephant and the camel have a mouth, legs, and a belly to receive food, so too for the mosquito and the moth.
>
> *Marpe Lenefesh*: Each Creator would have created different creatures which are not at all similar to the creatures of the other, and each Creators' works would have demonstrated a different form of wisdom, so that all can recognize that it is from a different Creator. But now that we see that they are all similar to each other - it must be that one Wisdom made all of them.
> Translator: All known living things are closely related. For example, they all, share a similar DNA system. Likewise, even the simplest bacteria are enormously complex and are given the poor scientists quite a run for their money. For the more they study, the more and deeper the complexity they confront (even for the "simplest" bacteria), and the more they are baffled by the divine wisdom before them.

Furthermore, we find that it is interdependent for its maintenance and welfare, no part is completed without the help of another part, like the links in a coat of armor, the parts of a bed, the limbs of the human body, or other things which have interdependent parts for their functioning.

(*Marpe Lenefesh*: Every creation in the world depends on something else for its existence and welfare, plants and anything which comes from the ground needs water, and animals need both, and man needs all of them...)

Can you see that the moon and the planets need the light of the sun, and the earth needs the sky and the water, and that the animals need each other, and some species feed on other species, such as predatory birds, fish, and beasts of the forest all need each other? And Man's need for everything, and the rectification of everything through man (man gives a higher purpose to everything). Countries, towns, sciences and trades are interdependent (each country has special resources/skills unique to it - *TL*).

And the Divine wisdom appears in the tiny creatures as well as the large ones, because the wisdom manifested in the formation of an elephant, despite its huge body, is no more wondrous than the wisdom manifested in the formation of a tiny ant. On the contrary, the smaller the creature the more wisdom and power it appears to reflect, and the more it testifies to the wondrous ability of the Creator. (since its tiny limbs and sinews are more amazing due their small size than they are in the big creatures - *TL*)

This teaches that they are all the design of one Designer and Creator, since they are similar and alike in furthering and completing the natural order and maintenance of the world in all of its parts. If there were more than one Creator, the form of wisdom exhibited would be different in some of its parts, and things would not be interdependent. Since the world, despite its being different in its roots and foundations, it is equal in its derivatives and compounds, one can see that its Creator who put it together, its Governor, and Designer is one.

A philosopher once said: "no part of what G-d created is more wondrous than another part". Which means the wisdom in a tiny creature of this world is similar and equal to that in a large one, as David, peace be unto him, said: "O L-ord, how manifold are Your works! with wisdom have You made them all: the earth is full of Your possessions" (Ps. 104:24), and "O L-ord, how great are Your works! Your thoughts are exceedingly deep" (Ps. 92:6).

(Translator: Even in the tiniest segment of the inanimate

world, there is an infinite character of wisdom as the Nobel prize winning physicist Richard Feynman said (from his book: *The Character of Physical Law* - Chapter 2 - the relation of mathematics to physics):

"It always bothers me that according to the laws as we understand them today, it takes a computing machine an infinite number of logical operations to figure out what goes on in no matter how tiny a region of space, and no matter how tiny a region of time. How can all that be going on in that tiny space? Why should it take an infinite amount of logic to figure out what one tiny piece of space/time is going to do? So I have often made the hypothesis ultimately physics will not require a mathematical statement, that in the end the machinery will be revealed and the laws will turn out to be simple, like the chequer board with all its apparent complexities. But this is just speculation." End quote.

(Hence, in truth, the scientists don't grasp ANYTHING fully, because who can understand the work of G-d? If this is so for even the tiniest speck of empty space. How much more so, for an electron, or beyond to living organism, whose design is perfectly coordinated from the atomic level up. Go and see how scientists worldwide are dumbfounded at fully understanding even the simplest viruses which are far less complex than cells.

(*Michtav M'Eliyahu vol 3, pg.167*: "The scientists rely solely on what is detectable by the physical senses. Through this [scientific method] does one save himself from error or, on the contrary, he will fall in greater and more extreme error? Let us imagine: if a man receives letters from unknown people who come from different places. From one place, all the letters come written with green ink (since green ink is common there). From the second place, all the letters come in black ink. The letters are different in content. Those written with green ink are all full of nonsense and foolish matters. While those written with black ink are all words of wondrous wisdom.

An intelligent person will realize that the writers of the letters with wisdom are wise men. While the writers of the nonsense are fools. But a scientist will come and say: "I cannot say on the writers of the letters. For I cannot actually see them, much less can I say anything on their thoughts since it is concealed in their brains. Therefore, if I investigate their wisdom according to the content of the letters, this is not the scientific way. Rather, I am forced to examine their difference based on physical evidence that I can detect. Through this clear evidence, I will resolve the solution. Based on the evidence, I will hypothesize that the green ink is the cause of the foolishness in the letters from one place, while the black ink is the cause of the wise words from the letters of the other place.

So too, for the matters of our world. If we don't give thought to the inner side of the matter which is grasped by the heart (intuition), inside our soul, and we restrict our sight only to the superficial appearance of things, we will certainly not at all draw closer to the truth... we must look with an inner eye and look at the matter from all perspectives.

THE THIRD ARGUMENT

(*Tov Halevanon*: The scientist/rational investigator, from the role he assumes as rational investigator, it is his way to believe only that which he has clarified through logical proofs. While the "believer", who believes that which has not been clarified to himself through logical proofs, has already gone out of the role of "scientist/investigator" and has no business debating with them. And now that we are here today, and we have permitted ourselves to delve in the sea of rational investigation in order to clarify through logic the existence of G-d, to affix faith in Him in our hearts, in addition to the faithful tradition of our Torah. We have already attained an understanding of a logical proof of this, through which, out of love for Him, we can fix in our hearts.)

The third argument, from the chidush (non-eternal nature) which applies to the entire universe. Since our previous proofs demonstrated that the world is created (see chapters 5-6), it follows from this that it must therefore have had a Creator. For it is impossible for something to come into existence by itself. And when we see that a thing exists, and we are certain that at some time it did not exist - we will know through the testimony of a sound intellect that something other than itself created it, brought it into being, and formed it. (The intellect convinces our minds and testifies to us that it must be so, it is not possible in any way that there is not a Creator who created all that exists - *TL*)

Since we have established that the world has a Creator who created it and brought it into existence - we need not deliberate whether He is more or less than one since it is impossible for the existence of the world without at least one Creator. And if it were possible to conceive that the world could have come into existence with less than one Creator, we would consider this. But since we cannot conceive that something less than one can bring anything into existence, we conclude that the Creator must be one. Because in the case of things which were established through logical proofs, and the proof of their existence is impossible to deny - we do not need to assume more than what is necessary to account for the phenomena which the proof demonstrates.

> (*Pas Lechem*: Since the logical proofs necessitate the existence of one Creator, why and from where do we need to consider that He is more than one, since this logical proof on the existence of the Creator is completed and suffices also without more than one.
>
> *Tov Halevanon*: It is not proper for one to look to the ends of the earth, and consider more than what the proof requires him to believe in order to resolve the difficulties raised in his rational inquiry.

The analogy of this: When we see a letter of uniform handwriting and style (that the handwriting style and the spacing between letters and words is uniform from beginning to end - *PL*), it will immediately occur to us that one person wrote and composed it because it is not possible that there was not at least one person. If it were possible that it could have been written with less than one person, we would consider this possibility. And even though it is possible that it was written by more than one person, it is not proper to consider this unless there is evidence which testifies to this, such as different handwriting style in part of the letter or the like.

> (*Marpe Lenefesh*: If you see discrepancies in handwriting style, then you can say that perhaps two people wrote it due to the variation and the non-uniformity of the handwriting. But

all the time that you don't see any irregularity or non-uniformity, what pushes you to say that perhaps two people wrote it? - on the contrary, the fact that there is no irregularity testifies that one person wrote the entire letter.)

Since this is so (that we do not need to consider more than one Creator - *PL*), it is not necessary to know Him face to face, if this is not possible (just like it is not necessary to know the writer face to face in order to determine whether the letter was written by him alone or with someone else - *PL*), and it will suffice for us to see the letter, accepting as proof the writer's acts, namely, the form of the writing, instead of seeing the writer himself. From this, we will know with certainty that there exists a writer, who knows how to write and is capable of writing, who wrote this letter.

He did not partner with someone else in writing it. This we can see from its orderly form and uniform handwriting, since the work of two makers varies. It is not uniform and orderly in one manner, and it changes in quality and character.

(*Tov Halevanon*: Therefore when we see a legal document (in court), orderly and of uniform handwriting, behold there is a strong likelihood that only one writer wrote it, and we will judge the case assuming so. And if someone claims that it is the work of two scribes, the burden of proof will be on that person. And even though this is not a complete proof, nevertheless it is sufficient proof. Because it is not proper for us to ask a man to bring proofs and verify strange and remote possibilities, but rather only for normal and regular cases. The author will soon bring clearer arguments. He also brought this argument in order to strengthen the matter, like the usual way of investigators/philosophers.)

Similarly we will say regarding the Creator, since the signs of wisdom in His creations are similar and uniform, we must conclude that one Creator created them, and that without Him they could not have come into existence, although the Creator is not something that can be perceived either in Etzem (essence) or Mikre (incident). And since He cannot be seen, it is impossible to find Him and know Him except through the proofs and observations of His handiworks which point to Him. Then will our belief stand firm that He exists and that He is One, that He is Kadmon (eternal), who was and will be, the First and the Last, Mighty, Wise, Living.

> (*Pas Lechem*: He began with the title: "Mighty" because according to our understanding, He existed before everything, since immediately after we grasp that there exists a Creator who created the world from nothing, we will immediately recognize His Might, namely, the act of creating something from nothing... After this, when we reflect on the details of creation, and we study them and their parts - we will see signs of His wisdom and we will know that He is wise. Afterwards, we contemplate His providence in governing the world, we will know that He is living and among us always. Understand that all of these descriptions are obligatory and follow one after the other, with the creation of the world as their first source.)

Since He is not among the things which can be seen, the proofs regarding Him will stand for us in place of seeing Him.

> (*Pas Lechem*: That the rational proofs stood for us to bring us to believe in His existence, as if we had grasped what He is and as if we had seen Him... Perforce, we are forced to suffice with our limited grasp, by accepting the logical proofs instead of actually seeing Him because He is not among the things which can be seen.

Therefore, it is necessary for us to conclude that one Creator created the world, because the existence of created things is impossible without Him. The assumption of more than one God is superfluous and unnecessary. Therefore, one who claims this - his claim cannot be considered legitimate unless he brings a sound logical proof other than that which we have brought. But it is impossible to establish such a proof, since two sound logical proofs do not contradict each other (and we already brought sound proofs that He is one - *PL*).

All the evidence thus testifies on His unity, and negates the attributing to Him of any plurality, association or similarity, as G-d Himself declares: "Is there a god besides me?" (Isaiah 44:8), and "I am the First and I am the Last" (ibid 44:6), and "My hand has laid the foundations of the earth, and My right hand has spread out the heavens" (Isaiah 48:13), and "a just G-d and a Savior; there is none besides Me" (Isaiah 45:21).

(*Manoach Halevavot*: Since G-d is not visible, He wanted His handiworks to testify on His existence and wisdom. It is the way of a craftsman to desire that it be known that the craft was made by him. Therefore perforce He is one, because less than one is impossible and for more than one, the proofs don't hold, and all the evidence testifies only on one Creator..

Pas Lechem: "Plurality" refers to another of similar essence. "Association" refers to associating another in His deeds. "Similarity" refers to His deeds, namely, that none can make other deeds similar to His.

Translator: If you ask: I read on the news that scientists have created new living bacteria in the laboratory. Answer: if you research the claim, you will see that the scientists merely modified a living bacteria and then hoped it survived. Alternatively, their new "bacteria" does not grow and reproduce autonomously like actual living things. For to implement the latter is enormously complicated, requiring many systems such as energy, information, growth, import/export, transport, regulation, timing, etc. etc. We are nowhere near getting anywhere close to even making a blueprint for such a device. Way too many reactions and no known prototype other than the cell itself.

Just briefly, to get a feel for what even the "simplest" bacteria needs to do, let us consider the basic autonomous cell whose only task is to reproduce and synthesize the parts it needs from raw materials.

1. Information System - to build something which can reproduce and synthesize its own parts from raw materials requires a coordinated series of steps. Chemicals cannot do this. On their own, they just combine chaotically or crystallize into regular patterns such as in snowflakes. Hence, there must be information (ex. RNA or the like) storing the instructions to orchestrate the assembly.

2. Energy System - information by itself is useless. To

implement the instructions requires energy. A system that cannot generate or source energy just drifts chaotically or crystallizes into simple forms, forced to follow the path of least resistance. Hence, a system of producing or sourcing energy is necessary along with subsystems of distribution and management of that energy so that it goes to the proper place.

3. Copy System - in order to reproduce itself, the device must be able to implement the instructions of the information system using the energy system. This includes the ability to rebuild all critical infrastructure such as the information and energy systems and even the copy system itself.

4. Growth System - Without a growth system, the device will reduce itself every time it reproduces and vanish to zero-size after a few generations. This growth system necessitates subsystems of ingestion of materials from the outside world, processing of those materials, and assembling those materials into the necessary parts.This alone is a formidable chemical factory.

5. Transportation System - the materials must be moved to the proper places. Hence, a transportation system is needed for transporting raw materials and products from one place to another within the cell. Likewise, a system for managing the in-coming of raw materials and out-going of waste materials of all these chemical reactions.

6. Timing System - the growth system must also be coordinated with the reproduction system. Otherwise, if the reproduction occurs faster than the growth, it will reduce size faster than it grows and vanish after a few generations. Hence, a timing or feedback mechanism is needed.

7. Communication System - signalling is needed to coordinate all the tasks so that they all work together. The reproduction system won't work without coordination with the growth and power systems. Likewise, the power system by itself is useless without the growth and reproduction systems. Only when all the systems and "circuitry" are in

place and the power is turned on is there hope for the various interdependent tasks to start working together. Otherwise, it is like turning on a computer which has no interconnections between the power supply, CPU, memory, hard drive, video, operating system, etc - nothing to write home about.

Hence the "simple" task of reproducing and synthesizing parts is by no means simple. A cell is a marvelous entity no less mind-boggling than a full fledged organism. And this is just for the basic cell. Furthermore, all of this complexity is just for the basic cell. Consider for instance, all the processes that need to occur in the human egg cell after fertilization. It magnifies its size in only a few weeks or months thousand-folds and more. It self-organizes into some trillion specialized cells. What system known in reality is able to do so, only with mother's food and air digested and moved through the blood? Nothing like it even a tiny bit 1000 times exists anywhere ever. Such brilliant ability to magnify a structure by such an enormous factor, such sophistication and wisdom of creation - all autonomously in the womb.

REFUTATION OF ARGUMENT TO DESIGN
Parenthetically, one may come across "refutations" of the Argument from Design by the atheists/anti-theists out there along the lines of the following:

Things that look designed must have a designer - but designers look designed too. And designers are more improbable than the things they design. Hence, this premise is false.
As an illustration, my coffee mug looks designed, so it must have a designer. That designer was a production line, which is more improbable than the mug. A factory production line looks designed, so it must have had a designer. The designer was a team of human beings, which is more improbable than the production line. Human beings look designed, so they must have had a designer. That designer was G-d, which is more improbable than humans. G-d is the termination point of this regress, because nothing can be more improbable than G-d because G-d is Infinitely

Improbable. Since G-d is Infinitely Improbable, He is impossible and does not exist. Therefore, the original premise of the argument is false.

Answer: This argument is based on ignorance regarding what eternal implies. You cannot ask what designed something Eternal. By definition the Eternal always existed. The argument from design only applies to something we see cannot be eternal. If we see some intelligent design and we also know that it cannot be eternal, then we can reasonably conclude that it must have had a designer.

Human beings cannot be eternal (since they are composite, finite, etc.) therefore they must have had a designer. But G-d is eternal so we cannot ask what designed Him. We can say that we don't understand how something can be eternal. That's valid and correct, and it stems from our inability to understand and relate to the Eternal because we are non-eternal. On this, Maimonides wrote, "if I could understood Him, I would be Him". In truth though, when you think about it, the mystery is not "how can the eternal exist?", but rather "how can the non-eternal exist?".

To summarize, one cannot ask "what brought G-d into existence?" for in truth He is existence/reality itself as explained next argument...

THE FOURTH ARGUMENT

(*Translator*. Important Note. In this argument, we are talking about spiritual matters which are exceedingly deep. You can't think on them the same way you think on physical things. The author already warned in chapter 2 that only a select few can grasp these very subtle arguments. commentaries to follow!)

The fourth argument: We will say to anyone who thinks the Creator is more than one as follows. It must be that the essence of all these (supposed creators) is either one or not one.

If you say, that in essence they are one, if so, they are one thing, and the Creator is not more than one. (since certainly for the Etzem of one thing it is not applicable to attribute plurality - *PL*)

If you say that each one of them is, in essence, different from the other, it must therefore be there is some distinction between them due to their difference and non-similarity. If so, whatever is distinct is limited/bound. And whatever is limited/bound is finite. And whatever is finite is composite - and whatever is composite was brought into existence, and whatever is brought into existence must have a Creator.

Therefore, one who thinks the Creator is more than one must also assume that this creator was brought into existence. We already demonstrated, however, that the Creator is Kadmon (without beginning), and that He is the Cause of causes and the Beginning of all beginnings. Therefore, He must be one and as the verse says "You are the L-ord, You alone" (Nechemia 9:6). (end of proof)

> *some commentaries*
> (*Tov Halevanon*: there is a consensus that mikre (incident properties) do not apply to spiritual matters, (the nine attributes of mikre brought earlier): "Eich", "Kama" (brought earlier in this chapter), etc., because it is not relevant to speak of movement, place, or situation. Hence for spiritual things the only difference is in their Etzem/essence).
> "whatever is distinct is limited/bound" - i.e. any difference is a border. For once there is a difference between two things, namely, that one has something that is not in the other, this difference limits it in that it does not attain the matter in the other thing.
> "whatever is finite is composite" - i.e. you cannot have finiteness in something, namely, that its matter is different (less) than the other thing, unless it is the effect of some cause. And an effect is a composite of two matters. Firstly, its own existence. Secondly, from the aspect of its cause. Therefore, it is necessarily mechudash (non-eternal).
>
> *Manoach Halevavos*: The explanation of "limited/bound" is as follows. The matter of "limiting" something is to limit/bind it into its "type" and "difference". For example, a human being is a "living creature" that is "speaking". "Living creature" is its type which includes human beings, animals, and other living creatures, while "speaking" differentiates him from the animals and other living creatures. Hence, a man is necessarily composite of two things, namely, "type" and

"difference". This is what he meant by "whatever is distinct is limited/bound", i.e. anything separated out of a group must have some matter which is "different" between it and what it was separated from which distinguishes it. And anything distinguished between itself and something else must be similar to it in some respect, namely, the "type" which included them together... "whatever is finite is composite", i.e. since it has a "type" which includes it and a "border", namely, its "difference", if so, it is composite of "type" and "difference"... (see there)... This matter is exceedingly deep.

He brings the Moray Nevuchim Part 2, ch.2. which the Shem Tov Commentary there explains: "if there were two creators, then there would necessarily be some matter which they would share in common in their both being "creators". Because if we say there are here two human beings, it is necessary that these two human beings share in common the matter of "being human", and it must also be that there is some matter for which they are separated from each other. Because if they were not separated, then they would not be two. And if there is in each one something which is not in the other, then each one is a composite of two things (since each one has what it is in common with the other and what separates it from the other. [note that these are deep spiritual ideas and should not be looked at in physical ways.], and neither one can be the First Cause nor of necessary existence. Therefore, each one is subject to causes (i.e. is an effect of a cause)...)

Pas Lechem: If the Creator is more than one, it must be that each part (supposed creator) has its own etzem (essence) by itself. If so, we must say that there is a separation between them, namely, some boundary which separates between their etzem since they are split...if so, since there is a boundary between them which separates them, and behold, each one is limited, since each one does not spread out infinitely, since that would leave no existence for the second. Therefore each has an end and a limit, if so, each has the attribute of extent and spreading out since behold its limit is the extent of its spreading out, and anything which has the attribute of extent and spreading out can receive divisioning (i.e. it is not of infinite character), and whatever can receive divisioning is composed of parts, and anything composite must be brought into existence, as we clarified earlier, that the parts precede it. And anything brought into existence has a Creator since a thing cannot make itself..

Marpe Lenefesh: ... Here is a quote from the Rambam (Yesodei Torah 1:7): "This G-d is one. He is not two or more, but one... If there were many gods, they would have body and form, because like entities are separated from each other only through the circumstances associated with body and form. Were the Creator to have body and form, He would have limitation and finiteness, because it is impossible for a body not to be limited. And any entity which itself is limited and defined [possesses] only limited and defined power. Since our G-d, blessed be He, possesses unlimited power, as evidenced by the continuous motion of the spheres, we see that His power is not the power of a body. Since He is not a body, the circumstances associated with bodies that produce divisioning and separation are not relevant to Him. Therefore, it is impossible for Him to be anything other than one. The knowledge of this concept fulfills a positive commandment, as [implied by Deuteronomy 6:4]: [Hear, Israel,] The L-ord is our G-d, The L-ord is one." End quote.

(*Translator:* I had some email correspondence with a great Chasidish Torah scholar/teacher which sheds light on this exceedingly deep subject. Since this is an important part, I am including the transcript of our correspondence (Disclaimer: I cannot defend or guarantee the accuracy of his answers. Also note that he often puts words in quotes "like" "this" because he is careful not to utter or write any words which he deems are not completely true):

skip this correspondence
[QUESTION:] the Shaar Yichud of Chovot Halevavot says that whatever is not totally infinite must be composite and hence mechudash (created/not eternal). Cannot understand clearly why. can you please explain?

[ANSWER:] (filled in)

(Rabbi F.) Something which is not totally infinite has to have some kind of a border or limitation like beginning, end, etc.

As such it has a "measurement" of some sort and "size" and "dimensions" also of some sort.

As such - it has to be composite - at least from what it "is" and its "borders" of limitations/definitions/descriptions etc.

And as such - it has to be a result of a previous "something" that either "made" it or "shaped" it or "defined" it - something which CAUSED its "borders" to be what they are.

And if so - there has to be a point of "time" where it did not "exist" and then started to exist by the "definitions" of its "borders"/"limitations" and alike - i.e. not "everlasting" and "infinite" - but "mechudash" - something that showed up somewhere along the time axis as "new" (HKB"H (G-d) never showed up on the time axis C"V as "new" that wasn't there beforehand.).

End of "proof."

[QUESTION:] trying to understand this. but what it "is" and its "borders" seems to be within itself, no?

for example, a square has its area, and its borders (perimiter). but both are within the area of the square, so there is no real distinction between inside the square and its borders. so how is this a composite of itself and its borders?

[ANSWER:] (filled in)
(Me:) trying to understand this. but what it "is" and its "borders" seems to be within itself, no?

(Rabbi F.) that is the entire point (!) - for something truly Infinite - you are right - for something which is not - these are 2 different things - that is the whole point.

(Me:) for example, a square has its area, and its borders (perimiter). but both are within the area of the square, so

there is no real distinction between inside the square and its borders. so how is this a composite of itself and its borders.

(Rabbi F.) a square is a very general definition. There is infinite (really) number of possible squares. The specific borders derive the specific square. The "border" and "limit" the general concept into its specific measure. The "concept" and its "borders" are 2 separate entities.

[QUESTION:]
just to make sure I understand what you're saying, it sounds like anything finite is composite in that it was preceded by the framework which set its borders.

So it is not really composite by itself, just that it must be preceded by the framework which limits it, hence it cannot be eternal.

If so, it is composite in the sense that it needs a framework, not that it itself is composite in its constitution. For example, matter needs space, so space must precede matter. Is this correct?

[ANSWER:] (filled in)
(Me:) It sounds like anything finite is composite in that it was preceded by the framework which set its borders.

(Rabbi F.) yes.

(Me:) So it is not really composite by itself, just that it must be preceded by the framework which limits it hence it cannot be eternal.

(Rabbi F.) not exactly - once it is set with its borders - it is also "composite" by itself as well - it is intrinsic part of its "innate" "nature" - a "being" WITH "borders."

(Me:) if so, it is composite in the sense that it needs a framework, not that it itself is composite in its constitution. For example, matter needs space, so space must precede matter.

(Rabbi F.) correct in principle - WITH the correction above - matter is (obviously) composite in its "constitution."

(Me:) is this correct?

(Rabbi F.) now it is :)

[QUESTION:]
(I wrote earlier:) it sounds like anything finite is composite in that it was preceded by the framework which set its borders. (And you responded: "yes". kind of like saying an idea must be preceded by its inventor since the idea's existence depends on the inventor.)

so HBB"H is the framework of existence, or more precisely, existence itself, correct? (Hence, it is not relevant to ask "what created Him?" since He Himself is existence.)

If so, then why must He be infinite? Perhaps He is just infinite only in the sense that there is no existence besides Him. But perhaps existence itself is finite. Hence, HBB"H is everything, but everything is not necessarily infinite.
Like space. Space holds everything physical but it is not infinite (as he explained earlier and which I quoted in chapter 5).

[ANSWER:] (filled in)
(Me:) so HBBH is the framework of existence, or more precisely, existence itself, correct? (Hence, it is not relevant to ask "what created Him?" since He Himself is existence.)

(Rabbi F.) yes - HE is the existence - HE is the framework - and HE is the borders.

(Me:) if so, then why must He be infinite?

(Rabbi F.) because there is ONLY ONE TRUE MEANING of INFINITY - and this IS HE - so HE has to be INFINITE.

(Me:) Perhaps He is just infinite only in the sense that there is no existence besides Him.

(Rabbi F.) that is a built-in-contradiction!! "Infinite" in only "one" sense - or even in huge finite number of senses - is already a limitation that limits HIS TRUE INFINITY (which is in INFINITE ("number" of) senses).

(Me:) But perhaps existence itself is finite.

(Rabbi F.) existence of the creating is finite - HIS existence is INFINITE in ALL INFINITE ("number of") senses.

(Me:) Hence, HBB"H is everything,

(Rabbi F.) true.

(Me:) but everything is not necessarily infinite.

(Rabbi F.) if the line above is correct (and it is) - then this one cannot be correct.
"Everything" is INFINITE in HIS senses of "Everything" - the "everything" we know - even all the worlds etc. - it is NOT HIS EVERYTHING.

(Me:) Like space. Space holds everything physical but it is not infinite.

(Rabbi F.) NO - in this "comparison" the "container" and the "content" are both finite.
HBB"H as the "container" is INFINITE and the "CONTENT" (the worlds and the creations in them) IS finite.

[QUESTION:]
have been thinking alot about this border thing, and even asked around but nobody seems to know.

1. This whole idea that whatever is finite is intrinsically composite as a "being with borders".

normally the word "composite" is used to say something is

made up of two or more constituents. This "border" is not a "constituent" but sounds more like a conceptual idea.

Electrons or quarks for example, have no internal structure and are basically point-particles so they cannot have any kind of physical border encircling them. so what is their border? is it something tangible or is it just a concept?

For example two electrons are identical in every respect. the only difference between the two is that this one is not that one. is this what you mean by border?

Basically, I'm just having a very hard time understanding what this "border" is and how it is considered a "constituent" to make the thing a "composite".

[ANSWER:] (filled in)

(Me:) have been thinking alot about this border thing, and even asked around but nobody seems to know.

1. This whole idea that whatever is finite is intrinsically composite as a "being with borders". Normally the word "composite" is used to say something is made up of two or more constituents. This "border" is not a "constituent" but sounds more like a conceptual idea.

(Rabbi F.) correct - in a way - because truly - even an "idea" - IS a SPECIFIC "something" - "knowing" "something" is ALREADY "fitting" it into "frames" of words thoughts or anything that the soul uses in order to RELATE to "it."
So REALLY - the existence of a "border" and ANY type or sort - IS already 100% classified as "composite."

(Me:) Electrons
(Rabbi F.) not a good example - see further here. :)
(Me:) or quarks
(Rabbi F.) same comment.
(Me:) [Electrons] for example, have no internal structure and are basically point-particles so they cannot have any kind of physical border encircling them. so what is their border?

(Rabbi F.) they have numerous REAL borders - momentum -

speed - position - energy - spin - color - charge - mass - weight - SO many parameters (and more) that border them to be each one what they are!

(Me:) is it something tangible or is it just a concept?

(Rabbi F.) VERY tangible! - how else would you be able to write me this email (one out of "trillion" examples of how and where the knowledge of their borders (= and their characteristics) is known used and applied)?!

(Me:) for example two electrons are identical

(Rabbi F.) no.

(Me:) in every respect.

(Rabbi F.) no. see above

(Me:) the only difference between the two is that this one is not that one.

(Rabbi F.) no. see (again?) above

(Me:) is this what you mean by border?

(Rabbi F.) ANY level, type, sort, meaning, or aspect of "definition" your mind uses in order to relate to "something" (and watch the 5 words precisely chosen paralleling the 5 levels of kotz-Y-K-V-K).

(Me:) basically, I'm just having a very hard time understanding what this "border" is and how it is considered a "constituent" to make the thing a "composite".

(Rabbi F.) now hopefully less hard time and IY"H even EASY times!

(Me:) 2. I hear what you mean, that HBB"H is infinite and the creation is finite.

but how would you then define infinite?

(Rabbi F.) INFINITE is ONLY HBB"H - this is the ONLY
"definition" that one can apply with our limited finite language
and minds.
EVERYTHING else that uses this term is to start with a
"loan" - we "borrow" this word from HIM (with his generosity)
for essentially EVERY single FINITE concept - such a "built-
in" contradiction - the reason you on your own is able with a
blink of an eye to dismiss the stupidities of the goyim as you
do it so well below (and so did the KUZARI king! What a
SMART guy he was!).

(comment: As a crude analogy, a video game has certain
characters, each one having certain properties, abilities, or
position on the screen, etc. These things must have been set
by a computer programmer. They cannot just exist eternally,
without beginning.

Hence, the only thing that can be Eternal (without beginning)
is that which has no properties or limitations in any way. It is
completely infinite and boundless in all respects. It has no
parts or boundaries. This is a completely different "kind" of
existence than anything we are familiar with. Anything else
which has some sort of limitation or property cannot be
eternal.)

[QUESTION:]
why can't we say the infinite framework is eternal and also
the finite "squares" inside it are also eternal.

[ANSWER:]
If you have a square - it has boundaries - correct?

If the square is infinite - does it have boundaries?

Of course not it is - infinite.

If the square is at any possible size - but finite - it had
boundaries - that define it - yes - of-course!

If it is finite - it has boundaries - if it is not finite - infinite - it has NO boundaries.

Obviously - square - is merely a - mashal (analogy) to everything - NOT - just - a "square".

It therefore seen - proven - to ANYONE who just has a minimal common-logical sense - that - the BOUNDARIES are always - GREATER - LARGER - BIGGER - BROADER - than - what's in them - in any number of dimensions! - even in math - in abstract structures and so-called by their spaces - their bounded spaces etc - ALWAYS - the boundaries - contain the space-volume-structure-etc!

Hence - there is no way for anything to be greater than its boundaries!

If HAVAYAH-EINSOF has boundaries even one - it means - the boundary - is coming - from something - greater - bigger! Therefore - its uniqueness - is limited - finite - enabling-permitting empty spaces or existence of another G-d - G-D-FORBID!

[QUESTION:]
Just a question about how "anything which is finite (i.e. is not everything) must be preceded by the framework of its existence."

Physicists claim, there's no space or time before the supposed "Big Bang" so finite and infinite does not apply. How does one answer this?

Also, there was no time before the supposed "Big Bang" so there is no notion of "before and after". How can one answer this?

Can we say that "precede" means its existence depends on the framework, hence the framework "precedes" it in some non-time sense?

[ANSWER:] (filled in)

*(Me:)*Just a question about how "anything which is finite (i.e. is not everything) must be preceded by the framework of its existence." *(Rabbi F.)* who "gave" it its "definitions" (name, title, descriptions, borders etc.)? This source is the framework which preceded its existence. *(Me:)*Physicists claim, there's no space or time before the supposed "Big Bang" so finite and infinite does not apply. How does one answer this?

(Rabbi F.) First - to *start with* - what you write is about a reality as perceived and described by the Torah - so it is obvious that you are coming from somewhere *very* different and that has its own world-perspectives and teachings - so you do not *really* owe anyone any "explanation" - you are not there to "excuse" yourself - as if what you write about and the "big-bang" are "equivalent" in their level of legitimacy.

Second - the "big-bang" is a theory where one of its assumptions is based on a certain and specific "narrow-minded" behavior of time - namely - <u>linearly</u>. The theory "insists" - on inserting a non-linear process in it - while keeping the time-ticks linearly - "squeezing" different amounts of events into the same "ticks" of time. The more you go "back" - the more you need to squeeze into smaller and smaller segments of time. It is inevitable - that there is a point of <u>singularity</u> where there are infinite amounts of "events" in zero amount of time! In equivalent words ("inversion" of the space-time coordinates) - it is like saying that there are finite amount of events within infinite time - precisely the concept of Creation. So how do they go around it - simply - they IGNORE the existence of the singularity - they have NO explanation for it WHATSOEVER except TOTALLY WILD and CRAZY ideas - ideas that they CANNOT EVER check OR prove - they get away from the singularity by "inventing" more and more of those crazy ideas - sounding so "beautiful" and "inspiring" ("free leap of the vacuum" "quantum leap" "strings and sheets" and so many others - totally far-fetched and assumptions - just in order to justify their ideas of the expanding universe - deceiving everyone that they "know" everything that happened after it began (which is also ALL FULL of assumptions and a composite structure of pieces of theories that have NO (!) continuity (!) between them - only MORE assumptions) - and no matter how close you can get to the singularity - you can never "reach" it - and they make you "believe" that because they *supposedly* "traced" everything back to the first 10^-35 of the "first second" or so (and that process itself is FULL of assumptions and holes) - then it means they "know" "everything" - where EVERY child that knows basics of math will tell you that no matter how "short" and "tiny" the time-interval - you can dissect it "infinite" amount of times and still remain with something finite. Even though it is small, but still there is infinite "ROOM" there for Infinite amounts of events - but they make you "believe" (and "suppress" by this the REAL problem) that if you are "SO" close - it must be that you actually "know" everything - while the truth is that this is NOT the case - they can't really hide the singularity and the fact that it IS their main unresolved problem.

(comment: i.e. no matter how close you are to the big bang, you are still infinitely far from explaining what happened at point zero.)

*(Me:)*Also, there was no time before the supposed "Big Bang" so there is no notion of "before and after". How can one answer this?

(Rabbi F.) there was time - "order of times" - no time in the sense of ticks we know now - but there was "order-of-times/events."
Namely, *sequence* of events did take place - even *before* the "time" when time as we know it began to "tick." This sequence of events (which are various type of process in the Infinite BB"H like the emanations of higher realms and even prior to it - definitions of certain borders levels etc. as part of certain levels of Infinity where elements of "measurements" of some sort were already part of it as preparation for the lower worlds etc. - these will also exist and take place *after* the end of the "ticking" era that we know from our *limited* borders of sensation and connection with Divinity.

We are in the "midst" of a limited era in which the borders and limitations are maximized. And part of it is the existence of the sensation of the "ticking" of time - [which is] one "certain" type of "time-sensation." But there are more types of time - like above - sequence of events priorities first and last order of things etc. - which are different types of time - something the "science" obviously does not include in its "definitions" and is using just *one* type of time as if it is the only type of time. All the other types of time are not limited to the physical existences and the "ticking"-type-of-time. They are all Infinite in nature (and from them descended the very limited and specific type of *our* "ticking"-time). Science "insists" on and can deal only with the "ticking"-time - and even that, it knows how to deal with it *only* in a *linear* manner - one of the causes for its false description of the "universe" - its size and its date etc.

Trying to argue with them *from* their own limited system is like trying to explain to a creation that lives on a curved surface which is extremely small relative to the curvature and thinks and even measures its world as flat - even though it isn't. Only from a hugely bigger "astronomical" perspectives is when you can see that the curvature actually is the true description.

In a way - phenomenon related to the theory of relativity in very high speed did to our concept of time a similar change in terms of *high* speeds - *much* higher than the speeds we live in and experience - speeds that do not exist in daily life (except the light) that for many years were counted as "infinite." When these speeds were acknowledged as "high but finite" instead of "infinite" - countless realizations of the curved behavior of time and space were revealed to the human mind to see that our reality is not at all linear - it is only a good linear approximation for very very low speeds.

And yet - for all practical senses and even when knowing all these facts - for essentially almost all humans - these curved behavior of space and time are all totally foreign and unaccepted as if it is a fantasy mamash.

The same idea but different is true regarding the nature of
time as "ticking" being part of much broader concepts of time
which are different in nature - and only in very very "low"
"speeds" of time (i.e. "ticking") - it appears as the "only" type
of time. However - if time were to "tick" faster than we are
used to - *much, much* faster - our consciousness will be
open to naturally see the broader meaning of time and its
INFINITE "curve" and nature - something that the limited
concepts of it, including accepting its pace of ticking as
"constant" "eternal" and "axiomatic" by the limited scientists -
are merely "linear" approximation of the actual truth.

(Me:) Can we say that "precede" means its existence
depends on the framework, hence the framework "precedes"
it in some non-time sense?

(Rabbi F.) I believe that the above "teaching" covers *and*
explains the meaning of the "yes" to this question. Good for
you to think in this manner!
END OF THREAD

In a separate correspondence, a friend of mine asked him
the question: "How can I remember (or even better -- be
naturally motivated) to ask G-d for help throughout the day?",
he answered:

(Rabbi F.) with the thought that HE is the ONLY ONE, that is
the ONE and ONLY - i.e. there are those that are only one of
them (like people - each one there is only one) - namely -
there are those that are one but not the only one because
there are others that are also people - but HBB"H is not only
ONE - but he is truly the ONE and ONLY ONE - NOTHING
like it exists. This is why HIS "existence" as the Sages call it
is INTRINSICALLY NOT as all other existences - that HIS
PRESENCE is NOT like any other presence - and therefore
HIS EXISTING PRESENCE is ALWAYS there to speak ask
and communicate - in INFINITE (!) ways and forms that are
ALWAYS available to one that seeks it truly with his kavanah
and knowledge of HIS BEING as the ONLY BEING.
END OF ANSWER

With these introductions, we will understand the following passage in the Tanya (Likutei Amarim ch.22): "However, The nature of G-d is not like that of a creature of flesh and blood. When a man utters a word, the breath/sound emitted in speaking is something that can be sensed and perceived as a thing apart, separated from its source... But with the Holy One, blessed be He, His speech is not, separated from His blessed Self, for there is nothing outside of Him, and there is no place devoid of Him. Therefore, His blessed speech is not like our speech."
Back to the Shaar Yichud...

THE FIFTH ARGUMENT

The fifth argument, from the concepts of plurality and unity as follows.
In his book, Euclides defined unity as: "Unity is that property through which we say of any thing that is one". This means that by nature, unity precedes the individual thing, just as we say that heat precedes a hot object. If there were no "unity", we could not say of anything that it is one.

> (*Marpe Lenefesh*: If we see some unity and we call it "one", it must be that there is something else which exists whose unity is absolute, and from which stems this characteristic to also call the thing we see as a "unity", as we say on an object which is now hot, that there must be something intrinsically hot (fire/energy) from which it received its warmth, and that we also call "hot", as he will explain later)

The idea which we need to form in our mind of unity is of oneness that is complete, a uniqueness, that is absolutely devoid of composition (that we cannot join anything to this unity - *ML*) or resemblance (there is nothing similar to Him - *ML*). Free, in every respect of plurality or number, that is neither associated with anything nor dissociated from anything.

> (*Pas Lechem*: since association or dissociation only applies to things with some form of similarity, but He is the singular Unity which has no resemblance in any form whatsoever.

Marpe Lenefesh: No "number" means the concept of
numbers does not apply to this unity, since it is absolute unity
which has nothing after it. But if we describe Him as "one",
we would be standing by Him since "Ein Od Milvado" (there
is nothing besides Him), because if there were other things
like this, we would be able to count them, hence the true
Unity has no number. The idea of plurality is the opposite of
this...)

The idea of plurality is that of a sum of unities. Plurality therefore
cannot precede unity of which it has been formed. If we conceive
something plural with our intellect or perceive it through our senses,
we will know with certainty that unity preceded it, just like when
counting things, the number one precedes the rest of the numbers.
Whoever thinks the Creator is more than one, must therefore
nevertheless concede that there was a preceding unity, just as the
numeral one precedes the other numbers, and just like the notion of
unity precedes that of plurality. Hence, the Creator is absolutely
One, and Eternal (Kadmon), and none is Eternal but He as written:
"Before Me no G-d was formed, nor shall any be after Me" (Isaiah
43:10).

(*Tov Halevanon*: The number one precedes all of them since,
for two things, there is something which precedes them by
nature, namely, unity. And that which is Eternal (without
beginning) cannot have any matter whatsoever preceding it.

THE SIXTH ARGUMENT

The sixth argument, from the Mikre (incidental) properties that
attach to everything that is plural. Plurality is an incidental property
ascribed to the Etzem (essence), and comes under the category of
"Kamus" (quantity). Since He is the Creator of essence and
incident, none of these attributes can be ascribed to His glorious
Being. For, it having been clearly demonstrated through scripture
and reason that the Creator is above and beyond all comparison
with, and similarity to, any of His creations, and seeing that plurality
which adheres to the essence of anything that is plural is an
incidental property - this property cannot be fittingly ascribed to the
Creator's glorious Essence. And if He cannot be described as
plural, He must certainly be One because there is nothing in
between the two possibilities, as Chana said: "There is none holy as

the L-ord: for there is none beside You" (Shmuel I 2:2).

THE SEVENTH ARGUMENT:

If the Creator were more than one, then either each one of these hypothetical creators is capable of creating the universe by itself or could not have done so without the help of the other.

If any one of them is capable - the other Creator is superfluous, since the first is capable without him and does not need (the help) of the other. (and since he is not needed, and there is no evidence for more than one Creator, why should we be in doubt or be concerned for his existence? - *PL*)

And if the creation of the world cannot be completed without their partnering together, then no single one of them had full and complete strength and capacity. Each lacked the necessary power and ability and was weak. What is weak is finite in strength and essence. What is finite is bound. Whatever is bound - is composite. Whatever is composite has been brought into existence, and anything brought into existence must have some one who brought it into existence (a Creator).

Hence, what is weak (finite) cannot possibly be Eternal since the Eternal does not fall short in any respect nor stands in need of another's help. Therefore, the Creator is not more than One.

> (*Tov Halevanon*: This proof was similar to the fourth proof, except that there he built the proof from the matter of difference or boundary that must exist between them. There, he did not get into the matter of finiteness but instead came from the aspect of difference and border. Here he started from the argument of finiteness, namely that its power must be finite, and then ended with the argument of border - because it's all the same thing. (i.e. its a different way of saying the same thing). He repeated it [differently] to strengthen it and impress it in the mind of the reader.

If it were possible for the Creator to be more than one, it would also be possible that there would be disagreement between them in the creation of the world and that the matter would not have been completed. Since we find that all of this world follows one order, and a uniform movement for all of its parts, which does not change over generations nor does it seem to change in the nature of its conduct, therefore, we know that its Creator and Ruler is One, and that none besides Him alters His work or changes His rule, as scripture says: *"And who, as I do, shall call, and shall proclaim it, and set it in order for Me" (Isaiah 44:7)*, and David said: *"Forever, O L-ord, your word is stands fast in heaven; Your faithfulness is unto all generations: You have established the earth, and it abides" (Ps. 119:89-90)*

The Creator's perfect governance which we observe in His creatures (also indicate His unity - Rabbi Hyamson). For government can be perfect and abidingly consistent, smoothly in one way only when there is a single individual making decisions and conducting the matter, as in the king ruling a country or in the soul controlling the body.

Thus Aristotle said in his book on the subject of unity: "it is not good to have many heads, but rather to have only one head". So too Solomon said: "For the transgression of a land many are the princes thereof" (Mishlei 28:2).

> *Pas Lechem*: That when the people are rebelling and sinning to G-d, G-d will appoint on them multiple rulers, and automatically the governance will fail and the country will fall apart and be ruined...as in the second temple era where the governance fell in the hands of 3 strong rulers...as mentioned in the book of Josephus until the land became corrupted and destroyed through them.
>
> If we had evidence of any disagreement in the creation or conduct (ex. laws of physics change sometimes) of the world, it would be possible to suspect that perhaps there is a second G-d...

What we brought here should be enough for the understanding person (and not stubborn to hang on to wings of stubbornness and far off, stretches of the imagination answers - *TL*), and this should suffice to answer the believers of dual gods or the trinity gods of the Christians, and others. For when we establish the unity of the Creator of the world, all those who claim that He is plural will be automatically refuted (since in clarifying the unity there are no difficulties and no far off answers - *TL*). Note it well.

*** CHAPTER 8 ***

The distinction between true (absolute) unity and conventional unity is as follows.

> *Tov Halevanon* - *"conventional"* (lit. passing) - that this term is said in passing only, without intent of its precise meaning.

The term "one" is derived from the concept of "unity". The term is used in two senses. One of them is mikri (incidental), which is the conventional unity. While the second is in essence and enduring - this is true (absolute) unity.

> *Tov Halevanon* - For example, one man does not have absolute "unity" due to his being joined and composite of many parts. But he has some unity relative to two people
>
> *Tov Halevanon* - *Mikre* (incidental) is something which is not essential for the thing and it can exist without it, sometimes it is attached to it and sometimes not, while something which is in its essence is found on it always.

Incidental unity subdivides into two divisions. In one of these the character of multitude, collectivity, and aggregation is apparent in it, such as one genus which includes many species or like one species which includes many individuals, and like one man which is comprised of many parts or one army which includes many men.

Or like we say one Hin (measure), one Rova (measure) or one liter (ex. of rice or water) which contain smaller measures, each of which is also called "one" (even though each smaller measure can be broken down further - *TL*). Every one of these things we mentioned are called "one" conventionally, because the things included under the one name are alike. Every one of them may also be called "plural" since it includes many things which when separated and isolated will each be called "one". Unity in all these manners we mentioned is *Mikre* (incidental). Each is a unit from one perspective and plural from another aspect. (The term "absolute unity" does not apply to it since from one perspective it is correct to refer to it as plural - *PL*)

The second division of incidental unity is the unity attributed to a single individual, who though seemingly not plural and not a collection of several things, yet is essentially plural, - being composed of matter and form, essence and incident, susceptible to "creation" and "destruction", division and combination, separation and association, change and variation. (see commentaries)

Plurality must be attributed to anything for which any of these things we mentioned applies to, for they are contradictory to unity. Unity ascribed to anything essentially plural and variable in any way is undoubtedly *Mikre* (an incidental property) (not in its essence - *PL*). It is unity conventionally, but not in a true sense. Strive to understand this.

> *Pas Lechem "it is susceptible to creation and destruction"* - if so it changes from one form to another since it goes through many forms in its formation and likewise in its destruction until it ceases completely, as is known. Its formation is not completed suddenly in one instant. Likewise, its destruction does not occur suddenly without stages, one form to another. Hence, it is correct to ascribe to it plurality, since it necessarily has a "beis-kibul" (ability to receive) all of its potential stages. understand this.
> *"division and combination"* - i.e. that the thing can be divided. Hence, one can divide it or leave it as is in its assembled state. This is from the aspect of itself.
> *"separation and association"* - is from the aspect of relative to something else. That it can be separated from it by distance or associated with it by being in close proximity...

True (absolute) unity is also of two kinds. The first in abstract thought and the second in actual reality.

The abstract thought version is numerical unity, namely, the root and beginning of all numbers. It is the sign and symbol of a beginning unprecedented by any other beginning. For every true beginning is termed "One", as for example: *"And there was evening and there was morning, one day" (Gen. 1:5)*. Instead of saying "the first day", the verse uses the term "one (day)", because the term "one" refers to any beginning unprecedented by any other beginning. When repeated, it is called "the second", and when repeated again - "the third", and so on until the number "ten", "a hundred", "a thousand", which are also units of new series, and so on to infinity.

(*Pas Lechem*: In his fine words, he incidentally answered the question of Rashi in Genesis 1:5, who asked: "according to the order of creation, the verse should have said 'first day', but according to the author's words, the intent of the verse was to teach on absolute creation, which was the beginning of everything, including time...

"the first abstract and the second actual" - the first is unity grasped conceptually in the mind, not associated with any real object. The second is unity on something which actually exists. This only applies to the Creator, as he will explain.

"numerical unity, namely the root and beginning of all numbers" - "one" is the root of all counts since every count is comprised of a sum of ones. Hence, "one" is the root and foundation on which one builds a counting. It is also the beginning of the count for it is impossible for a counting not to start with one.

Tov Halevanon: The "one" with which we count some number is itself not really a number, because a "number" is basically: the grouping together of matters. And also, "one" never makes plurality, as you say "one multiplied by one", "one multiplied by two", everything remains unchanged, unlike the number two and above which always multiplies over, since two multiplied by two is four, two by three is six, and similarly for all numbers. Therefore "one" is only the foundation of numbers and the sign of beginning....there is nothing truly one besides G-d, if so, perhaps this term was borrowed to refer to a beginning without prior beginning. Likewise the Midrash Bereishis Raba says: "the verse did not say 'the first day', but rather 'day one', to teach on the unity of G-d")

Therefore the definition of number is that it is a sum of units. The reason I called it "abstract thought" is because the notion of number is not perceived by the physical senses. Rather, it is grasped only in thought. It is the "numbered" object (ex. eggs, nuts - *PL*) alone which is perceptible to the five senses or by some of them.

Pas Lechem: *"perceptible to the five senses or by some of them"* - some things are perceptible to all the senses. For example, a goat has an appearance perceived by the sense of sight, a sound perceived by hearing, a taste, when eating its meat, an odor by the sense of smell, and a texture to the sense of touch. Some things are perceived only by some senses such as an apple which is not perceived by the sense of hearing. A rock is perceived only by sight and touch.

The second kind of true unity exists actually. It is that which is neither plural nor susceptible to change or variation, is not described by any of the corporeal attributes, is not subject to "creation" (rather He is Kadmon/without beginning - *TL*), destruction or end. Does not move (from place to place - *TL*) or waver (this refers to any change whether in *Etzem*/essence or *Mikre*/incident - *TL*), does not resemble anything nor does anything resemble it, and is not associated with anything. It is from all possible perspectives - true Unity and the root of everything plural. For as we already pointed out, unity is the cause of plurality.

(*Pas Lechem*: "nor susceptible to change or variation" - it is not correct to ascribe to the true unity any change from one form to another, nor is it correct to ascribe variation to say it is the opposite of something else... a rock for example, cannot be termed "speaking" nor can it be termed "mute". So too, for the true Unity, it is incorrect to associate it with anything nor to say it is the opposite of something.

"not described by any corporeal attribute" - such as anger, mercy, etc. whatever is said of Him is only metaphorical, as is known.

destruction or end - he added "end" because there exists some things which don't become destroyed but they end, such as a specific time. It is incorrect to say that time was destroyed, but rather to say it was completed and ended.

"It is, from all possible perspectives - true Unity" - i.e. from all possible perspectives of plurality that we turn to, we find Him completely devoid of it.

Tov Halevanon: "does not resemble anything" - That He has no comparison whatsoever to any of His creations. For example, for one grain of sand versus the universe and everything in it, even though this is extremely tiny and this is extremely big, nevertheless there is a comparison between the two and a shared characteristic...and the difference between them is only in size, but relative to Him, one cannot make any comparison by any trait or measure, just like one cannot compare a voice to a picture)

The true unity has neither beginning nor finiteness because anything which has a beginning or finiteness necessarily must be subject to origination and destruction. And anything subject to these is also subject to change, and change is inconsistent with Unity. Hence, it would be more than one since it had existed as one thing and then changed into a different thing, and this necessarily implies plurality.

(*Tov Halevanon*: A thing which changes must have two powers, namely, the power that it is now, and the power for that which it has the potential to become, and this contradicts unity.

Pas Lechem: Anything which changes must have had plurality in its first state, because it had two powers, one: what it was, and two, the beginning [potential] for the second existence which it changed into, and it is so that the philosophers agree that anything which changes had the potential for change inside it from the beginning, since if this is not so, from where did it come out afterwards to actuality? because that which is not in potential will never go out to actual. The commentators already expounded this from the verse "the day of death from the day of birth" (Eccles. 7:1). If so, behold, it has two powers, namely the previous entity and the beginning for the second entity, and it is not one.. Understand this.)

Similarity is also an incidental property (mikre) in anything which is similar (to something else), and whatever has an incidental property is plural. But absolute unity, in its glorious essence, is not subject to any incidental properties whatsoever in any respect.

Pas Lechem: "similarity" - A comparison term which is ascribed to the bearer of that comparison, that it is called "similar" to - it is *Mikre*, because it is attached to the *Etzem* (essence) of the bearer of that term.

"whatever has an incidental property is plural" - since behold it has essence and incident (2 things).

Tov Halevanon: If we say, for example, that Reuven is similar to Shimon, this comparison that we are comparing Reuven with is an "incident" that occurred to Reuven, that he is similar in that respect... Anything which has *Mikre* is considered more than something else, because *Mikre* is something which is added to the *Etzem* (essence) of that thing.

If one will claim that the quality of "unity" is itself an incidental property in the Absolutely One.

Tov Halevanon: It is possible to ask - How can we say on G-d that He is the absolute unity. Behold, this is also *Mikre*, it is a type of numerical property which is also ascribed to physical things. i.e. they are ascribed the incidental property of number, namely the number one, two, etc. If so, the true unity is also an incidental property and something additional attributed to His essence, and this is also plurality.

We will answer this as follows: The ascribing of true unity is intended to express the exclusion of multitude and plurality. When we describe Him as One, we mean only the negation of any multitude or plurality. But the true Unity, cannot be described by any attribute that would connote in His glorious essence any plurality, change, or variation. With this we have completed our words, regarding the true unity and the relative unity. Note it well.

Pas Lechem: We are not ascribing to Him unity, just negating the opposite, namely plurality. Likewise, the intent for any "attributes" we ascribe to Him such as "Living", "Wise", "Powerful" is only to negate the opposite.

*** CHAPTER 9 ***

> *Tov Halevanon:* he will now clarify that the Creator is the true
> Unity, in addition to what he clarified in chapter 7 that the
> creator is one)

The proof that the Creator is the true (absolute) Unity and that there
is no true Unity besides Him is as follows.

Any composite thing only comes completely into existence when the
parts of which it is comprised join together and unite. The
association (of the parts) is the unity.

And likewise, the existence of something composite is not possible
without the (possibility of - *TL*) dividing (or disintegrating) the parts
of which it is comprised, since composition necessarily implies more
than one part. The divisioning of the parts is plurality.

And since the signs of composition, synthesis, and arrangement are
found in the universe as a whole as well as in its details and parts,
in its roots and derivatives, it is necessarily subject to synthesis and
division, and must contain the basic principles of Unity and Plurality.

And since, in essence, Unity precedes Plurality, just like the number
one precedes the other numbers, it follows that the First cause of
everything that is plural, which was at the head of all beginnings is
itself not plural since all things plural are preceded by unity.

> (*Tov Halevanon:* - The head of all beginnings cannot possibly
> be plural, since if it were plural, then unity must have
> preceded it, and we already said that He is the head of all
> beginnings.

And since causes must reach a limit at their beginning, and it is not
possible for a thing to make itself, therefore it is impossible for the
cause of unity and plurality to itself be of unity and plurality like them
(since that would necessitate another unity that preceded it - *TL*)

And since the First Cause of the creations cannot itself be plural nor
a combination of plurality and unity, it must necessarily be that the
Cause is a true (absolute) Unity.

(*Manoach Halevavos*: It is not possible for the cause of unity and plurality to be unity and plurality like them since anything which has unity and plurality, namely, unity from one side and plurality from the other - is composite, and every composite is mechudash (created) and necessitates another maker since a thing cannot make itself)

And we have already demonstrated that the more one ascends the succession of causes, the fewer the causes will be until eventually the root of all numbers is reached - this is the true Unity, and this true Unity is the Creator.

(the following is another proof - *TL*)
Furthermore, it is known that anything which is found in something as an incidental property must also exist in something else as its true essence and cannot be separated from that (something else) without destroying it. For example, hotness, an incidental property of hot water, is the permanent essence in fire. Or, moistness, an incidental property in various objects, is permanent essence in water.

(*Marpe Lenefesh*: hotness can only leave the fire if the fire is completely destroyed because it is in its essence whereas for hot water, even if the hotness leaves the water, the water remains in existence because the hotness was in the water only as an incidental property)

And it is known that anything which is found in an object as an incidental property, that object must have received the incidental property from something else for which that incidental property is in its essence, such as hotness in hot water which is incidental in the water. It was given to the water from fire whose hotness is in its essence or some other energy source. And when we see moisture in moist things as an incidental property, we know that it was transferred to them from water whose wetness is in its essence. Similarly for all things, if we examine their matters.

Pas Lechem: Any quality that we find in a subject as an incidental property, namely, that it is not a quality in its essence but rather only an incidental property attached to it, we will know for certain that this quality must be found in another subject as a true name reflecting its essence. Since the quality is "essence" in that thing its name is called on it in truth, not as a borrowed, passing term. Therefore, it is called its true name.

He brought as an example, hotness in hot water, that even if we never saw fire but only saw hot water and we know that hotness is not an "essence" property in water and is just acquired and attached to it from outside - from this we would understand that there must exist something for which hotness is a quality in its essence and from there the water acquired this property as an incidental property, namely, from fire (note: one can heat water without fire, for example through friction or radiation. I think he means here the foundation of fire which is general manifested energy)

Through this principle we can direct our words to the matter of unity. Since unity is found in every created thing as an incidental property, as we introduced, it necessarily follows that it must be a true and permanent essence in the Cause of all created things, and from it all created things derived the matter of unity as an incidental property, as we explained.

When we investigated the matter of true (absolute) unity among the created things, we did not find it to be absolute or permanent in any of them. If we try to apply it to any of the sugim (types, i.e. broad category such as animals), minim (kinds, categories of a type such as horses), ishim (individuals, subcategories of kinds such as one individual horse), Etzemim (essence of things), (mikre) incidental properties, planets, stars, spiritual bodies (angels, he called them "bodies" since they are also of limited power - PL), numbers, numbered objects, (to summarize) anything which is finite and limited, and we try to call it one, and try to ascribe the term "unity" to it - this we cannot correctly do to call it "one" except in a passing (relative) sense. For each of them comprises things which are collectively called "one" due to their similarity and joining together in one respect.

But essentially, each of them is plural, being subject to multitude and change, division and separation, association and dissociation, increase and diminishment, motion and rest, appearance and form, and other incidental properties, whether specific to it or general that belongs to every creation.

(*Pas Lechem*: For example, appearance, form and change is specific to physical things of our world and do not apply to spiritual creations in the (higher) spiritual worlds... However the general incidental property of plurality and finiteness applies to all things except G-d.

Absolute Unity is not found nor truly ascribed in any created thing. And since unity exists among the created things as an incidental property, while all the evidence points to the Creator being One, we will deduce with certainty that the relative unity that we ascribed to any of the created things emanates from the true (absolute) One. And this true (absolute) unity can only be ascribed to the Creator of all. He is the true One. There is no true (absolute) Unity besides Him.

All the implications of absolute Unity we have mentioned befit Him alone. All the matters of plurality, incidental properties, change, motion, comparison, or any qualities which is not consistent with true Unity cannot be ascribed to Him, as David said: "Many, O L-ord my G-d, are Your wonderful works and Your thoughts towards us, there is no comparison to You" (Ps. 40:6), and "To whom then will you liken G-d? Or what likeness will you compare unto Him?" (Isaiah 40:18), and "Among the gods (angels) there is none like unto You, O L-rd; neither are there any works like unto Your works" (Ps. 86:8).

It has been clarified and demonstrated that the Creator of the world is the true Unity and that there is no other true Unity besides Him. For anything which is ascribed the term "one" besides the Creator, is a unity from one aspect but plural from another aspect. But the Creator is one from every respect as we explained. What we have brought in this matter should be sufficient for the intelligent person.

*** CHAPTER 10 ***

> (*Tov Halevanon*: After he brought proofs that G-d is the true
> Unity, he returns to clarify that G-d has no plurality from the
> view of the attributes of praise and good traits with which we
> praise G-d and which are found in scripture...)

(Translator: Rabbi Moses Hyamson's translation was heavily
consulted here and in the previous few chapters due to the difficult
language)
Regarding the Divine attributes, whether known from reason or from
scripture, which are ascribed to the Creator - the intentions in them
are numerous according to the numerous creations and the
kindnesses bestowed on them.

They (the Divine attributes) divide into two divisions: Essential (in
essence) and Active (i.e. from His deeds).

> (*Marpe Lenefesh*: Some attributes are in Him as etzem
> (essence), even if He did not create the world, while others
> we call Him due to His deeds)

The reason we call them Essential (in essence) is because they are
permanent traits of G-d, belonging to Him before the creations were
created, and after their creation these attributes continue to apply to
Him and to His glorious essence.

These attributes are three:
1. That He (permanently) exists
2. That He is One
3. That He is Eternal, without beginning.

> (*Pas Lechem*: Even after the creation no existing thing can
> be associated with Him in these three attributes...they can be
> ascribed exclusively to His glorious essence, unlike the
> "Active" attributes that the creations can associate with them
> a bit, as will be explained, and as the Sages say (Shabbat
> 133b): "cling to His ways, just like He is merciful so too be
> merciful, just like He is gracious, so too be gracious, etc.")

We ascribe to Him these three attributes and speak of them in order
to indicate His Being and true existence, to call attention to His

glory, to make human beings understand that they have a Creator whom they are under duty to serve (as to the question of why should we serve Him if He lacks nothing and needs nothing, this will be explained in gates 2 and 3).

We must ascribe to Him "existence", for His existence is demonstrated by proofs based on the evidence of His handiworks, as written: *"Lift up your eyes on high, and behold who has created these things? He that brings out their host by number: He calls them all by name. By the greatness of His might, and for He is strong in power; not one fails" (Isaiah 40:26)*.

We must necessarily ascribe existence to Him because it is a principle accepted by our reason that for something which is non-existent no action or result can come. Since His works and creations are manifest, His existence is equally manifest to our intellect.

We ascribe to Him Eternity (no beginning), because rational arguments have demonstrated that the world must have a First (cause) which had no previous cause before it and a Beginning which had no prior beginning. It has been demonstrated that the number of causes cannot be infinite. It logically follows, that the Creator is the First Beginning before whom there is no Beginning, and this is what is meant by His Eternity, as written: *"From everlasting to everlasting, You are G-d" (Ps. 90:2)*, and *"before Me there was no god formed, neither shall any be after Me" (Isaiah 43:10)*.

Regarding declaring of Him that He is One, we have already sufficiently demonstrated this by well known arguments and it has been established by clear evidence, that true Unity is inseparable from His glorious essence. This unity implies absence of plurality in His Being, the absence of change, transformation, incident, origin or destruction, joining or removal, comparison or association or any other properties of things that are plural.

It is necessary for you to understand that these attributes do not imply any kind of change in His glorious essence, but only to denote a negation of their opposite. What the attribution of them should convey in our minds is that the Creator of the world is neither plural, nor non-existent, nor created (which are the opposites of unity, existence, and Eternity - *PL*)

Likewise it is necessary for you to understand that each one of these three attributes we mentioned implies the other two, when we analyze them. The explanation of this is as follows:
When true Unity is the inseparable and permanent property of a thing, that thing must necessarily also be Eternally Existing (without beginning), since that which is non-existent cannot be ascribed neither unity nor plurality. Hence if true (absolute) Unity is the attribute of any thing and essentially belongs to it, it logically follows that the attribute of Existence with its implications also belongs to it. It must also be Eternal (eternally existing) because true (absolute) unity neither comes into existence nor passes out of existence, neither changes nor is transformed. Hence, it must be Eternal, for it has no beginning (and no end, for what has no beginning is endless - Rabbi Hyamson). Hence, that which the matter of true Unity belongs has also the attributes of Existence and Eternity.

So too, we say that the attribute of permanent Existence, attributed to a thing, implies the attribution to it of absolute Unity and Eternity (without beginning).

> (*Manoach Halevavos*: "permanent existence" - this he derived earlier from the premises in chapter 5 that the world must have a Creator, for the number of beginnings cannot be infinite, and that a thing cannot make itself, hence the Creator's existence must be a permanent existence. For otherwise, how could He come to exist after He did not exist since a thing cannot make itself?)

It implies absolute Unity since that which permanently Exists could not have come into existence from nothing, and cannot pass from the state of existence into that of non-existence. Such a thing is not plural since that which is plural is not permanently existent, as it must have been preceded by Unity. Therefore, that which exists permanently is not plural, and is accordingly, One.

The attribute of Eternity (without beginning) also belongs to it, since that which exists permanently has neither beginning nor end, and is accordingly Eternal.

So too, we assert that the attribute of Eternity, belonging to any Being, also implies in that Being, the attributes of absolute Unity and permanent existence.

It implies Unity, since that which is Eternal has no beginning, and that which has no beginning is not plural, since all things plural have a beginning, namely, a (parent) unity. Therefore, that which is plural is not Eternal, and that which is Eternal can only be One. Therefore, the attribute of absolute Unity is implied in the attribute of Eternity.

Likewise, the attribute of existence is implied in that of Eternity. For the non-existent cannot be described as either Eternal or created.

We have clarified that these three attributes are one in meaning and imply the same thing. They do not imply any change in the Creator's glorious essence, nor do they imply any incidental property or plurality in His being, because all that we are to understand by them is that the Creator is neither non-existent, nor created, nor plural. If we could express His being in a single word which would denote all three of these attributes as they are understood by the intellect so that these three attributes would arise in our mind when the one word was used, we would use that word to express it. But since we do not find such a word in any of the spoken languages which would designate the true conception of G-d, we are forced to express it with more than one word.

This plurality in the Creator's attributes does not, however, exist in His glorious essence but is due to inadequacy of language on the part of the speaker to express the conception in one term. You must understand that, regarding the Creator, there is none like Him, and whatever attributes we speak of regarding Him, you are to infer from them the denial of their opposite. As Aristotle said "negating attributes of G-d gives a truer conception of Him than affirming attributes". For all affirmative attributes ascribed to G-d must necessarily ascribe properties of Etzem (essence) or Mikre (incidental properties), and He who created etzem and mikre has not the properties of His creatures in His glorious essence. But the denial of such properties to Him is undoubtedly true and appropriate to Him. For He is above all attributes and forms, similarity or comparison. Therefore, you must understand from these attributes that they refer to the negation of their opposites.

(*Marpe Lenefesh*: It is better to negate ascribing to the Creator attributes which are lackings on Him. For example, it is more correct to say that the Creator is not plural, not non-existent, not created, which are opposites, and which are more true than saying and affirming on Him that He is the "true Unity", "permanently existing", "eternal", because we are not capable of understanding what is true Unity,...)

THE ACTIVE ATTRIBUTES

The active attributes of G-d are those which we speak of the Creator with reference to His works. It is possible, when speaking of them, to associate Him with some of His creations. We were permitted, however, to ascribe these attributes to Him because of the forced necessity to acquaint ourselves with, and realize His existence, in order that we assume on ourselves the duty of His service.

We have already found that the Torah and the books of the Prophets extensively use these active attributes, as also in the Psalms of prophets and saints. They are used in two manners:

One, attributes which denote physical form such as in the verse "So G-d created man in His own image, in the image of G-d, He created man" (Gen. 1:27), "for G-d made man in His image" (Gen. 9:6), "by the word of G-d" (Numbers 9:18), "I, even My hands, have stretched out the heavens" (Isaiah 45:12), "in the ears of G-d" (Numbers 11:1), "under His feet" (Ex. 24:10), "the arm of G-d" (Isaiah 51:9), "who has not taken My soul in vain" (Ps. 24:4), "in the eyes of G-d" (Gen. 6:8), "G-d said in His heart" (Gen. 8:21), and other similar verses regarding physical limbs.

Two, attributes which denote bodily movements and actions, as written: "and G-d smelled the pleasing aroma" (Gen. 8:21), "And the L-ord saw...and the L-ord regretted" (Gen. 6:5-6), "and G-d came down" (Gen. 11:5), "and G-d remembered" (ibid 8:1), "and G-d heard" (Numbers 11:1), "Then the L-ord awakened as one out of sleep," (Ps. 78:65), and many more activities of human beings like these attributed to Him.

Our Rabbis, when expounding the scriptures, paraphrased the expressions used for this class attributes and were careful to render them in an honorable way, and ascribed them all to the "glory of the Creator". For example, the verse "behold G-d stood over him" (Gen. 28:13), they rendered - "the glory of G-d was present with him"; "and G-d saw" (ibid 6:5), they rendered - "it was revealed before G-d"; "and G-d came down" (ibid 11:5)- "the glory of G-d was revealed"; "and G-d went up" (ibid 35:13) - "the glory of G-d departed from him".

They rendered everything in a reverential way, and avoided attributing them to the Creator in order not to ascribe to Him any kind of physicality or incidental property.

The great master, Rabeinu Saadia, already expounded sufficiently at length on this in the Sefer Emunot Vedeot, in his commentary on parsha Bereishis, parsha Vaera, and in Sefer Yetzira, and we do not need to repeat his explanations in this book. What we are all agreed upon is that necessity forced us to ascribe physicality and to speak of Him with the attributes of His creations in order that human beings can have some way to grasp the existence of the Creator. The books of the prophets connoted Him with corporeal terms because these are closer to our mind and understanding.

If they had spoken of Him in a more accurate fashion, using words and matters connoting spiritual things, we would not have understood neither the words nor the matters, and it would have been impossible for us to worship something which we do not know, since it is not possible to worship an unknown. Therefore it was necessary that the words and concepts be according to the understanding ability of the listener so that the matter will first be grasped in the listener's mind in an understandable, corporeal sense from the concrete terms. Afterwards, we will enlighten him and explain to him that all this was only metaphorical, to bring the matter close and that the true matter is too fine, too sublime, too exalted, and too remote from the ability and powers of our mind to grasp. The wise thinker will endeavor to remove the husk of the terms and their corporeality and will ascend in his mind step by step until he will reach the true intended meaning according to the power and ability of his mind to grasp.

The foolish and simple person will conceive the Creator in accordance with the literal sense of the metaphor, and if he assumes the service of His Creator, and he endeavors to labor for His glory, he has in his simpleness and lack of understanding, a great valid excuse because a man is held accountable for his thoughts and deeds only according to his ability, intelligence, understanding, strength, and material means. But if the foolish is capable of learning wisdom and he neglects it - he will be held accountable for it and punished for his lacking and refraining from study.

If the scriptures had employed more accurate, truer terminology, then nobody would have understood it except the wise, understanding reader and most of mankind would have been left without religion and without Torah (guidance) due to their limited intellect and weak understanding in spiritual matters. But the word which may be understood in a material sense will not damage the understanding person because he recognizes its real meaning, and it is at the same time beneficial to the simple person so that it will fix in his heart and mind that there is a Creator which it is his duty to serve.

This is similar to a man who came to visit a friend who was of the wealthy class. His wealthy host felt a duty to provide his friend with a meal and also food for the animals which he brought with him. The wealthy man sent to him an abundant quantity of barley for his animals and a small quantity of food fitting for him but only enough for his need.

So too, the scriptures and the books of the pious abundantly employed material analogies when referring to the attributes of the Creator according to the understanding of the masses and according to the common language which the masses converse. Therefore, when referring to this, our Rabbis said "the Torah speaks like the common language of men" (Bava Metzia 31b). And the scriptures gave few hints of spiritual matters which are intelligible only to the (few) wise and understanding men.

In this way, even though all people have different views of G-d's glorious essence, nevertheless, all people are equal with regard to knowing the existence of the Creator (and that it is one's duty to serve Him - ML).

Likewise we will say for all subtle matters found in the Torah such as the reward in the next world or its punishment.

> (*Tov Halevanon*: Since the good reward cannot be understood by a foolish or a simple person. The crude cannot understand spiritual pleasure, only physical pleasures, and likewise only physical punishments. Therefore, the scriptures speak only of physical reward and punishment, and hinted in few places of spiritual reward and punishment)

And likewise we will say for the clarification of the inner wisdom (the duties of the heart) which was our intention to clarify in this book. The Torah was very brief in expounding their matters, relying on the intelligent men. The Torah only hinted at it to arouse one on it, such as mentioned in the Introduction of this book, so that anyone who is able to enquire and investigate them will be aroused to do so until he has understood and mastered them as written: "those who seek G-d will understand all things" (Mishlei 28:5).

> (*Manoach Halevavos*: For spiritual matters, the Torah gave few hints because this is only for the wise, and the truly wise have a single, common viewpoint, and all of them grasp exactly the same matter with only these few hints, according to what is fitting and possible for them, because the false and erroneous ways are numerous but there is only one way of truth.)

The prophet (Moshe Rabeinu) has already warned us against thinking that G-d has a form or likeness as written "Take therefore good heed unto yourselves; for you saw no manner of form on the day that the L-ord spoke unto you in Horeb (Sinai) out of the midst of the fire" (Deut. 4:15), and "And the L-ord spoke unto you out of the midst of the fire: you heard the voice of the words, but saw no form; only you heard a voice" (ibid 4:12). When saying "take good heed", he warned us in our minds and thoughts to not represent the Creator under any form (tavnis) or to conceive Him under the likeness (demus) of anything or any comparison (dimyon) since your eyes never perceived any form or likeness when He spoke to you.

> (*Pas Lechem*: "Tavnis" is the form. It is called "tavnis",

derived from the (similar Hebrew letters of the) word "binyan" (building), since the form is like a building, built from the assembly of specific parts according to a determined amount. This term is used for living creatures such as "tavnis of all fish" (Deut. 4:18), since they are built and synthesized from different organs/parts. And they are of form. This term is also used in buildings such as "tavnis heychal" (the form of the inner temple), unlike fire or wind where the term "tavnis" is not relevant to them since they don't have a specific form. It is only correct to employ for them the term "demus" (likeness), since they are grasped in likeness by a mirror. But G-d is beyond any form or likeness...and for other types of physical characteristics such as sleep, laughter, joy, sadness, or the like he said "dimyon" (comparison), that would make comparable through these acts to His creations. Understand this.)

And it is written "To whom will you liken to G-d? What likeness will you compare to Him?" (Isaiah 40:18), and "to Whom will you liken Me that I will be equal to, says the Holy One" (ibid 40:25)

(*Pas Lechem*: Behold not only is it beyond the power of man to conceive in Him a likeness but even G-d testifies on Himself that He has no connection whatsoever to any kind of likeness.)

And it is written: "For who in the heaven can be compared unto the L-ord?" (Ps. 89:7), and "Among the mighty ones there is none like You, O L-ord" (Ps. 86:8), and many more like this.

Since it is impossible to form a representation of Him with the intellect or picture Him with the imagination, we find that Scripture ascribes most of its praises to the "Name" of G-d (and not to His essence - *PL*), as written: "And they shall bless Your glorious Name" (Nehemiah 9:5), and "that you may fear this glorious and revered Name" (Deut. 28:58), and "Let them praise Your Name, great and revered" (Ps. 99:3), and "of My Name he was afraid" (Malachi 2:5), and "But unto you that fear My Name shall the sun of righteousness arise with healing in its wings" (Malachi 3:20), and "Sing unto G-d, sing praises to His Name, extol Him that rides upon the skies, whose Name is the L-ord" (Ps. 68:5).

All this is in order to honor and exalt His glorious essence because, besides clarifying that He exists, it is impossible for us to clarify in our minds anything about His Being except for His great Name.

> (*Pas Lechem*: Which the Torah has taught us that He is called by this Name... it teaches on the "revelation of His glory".
>
> *Marpe Lenefesh*: This is the "shem hameforash", the "shem haetzem" (name of essence), "this is My Name forever" (Ex. 3:15). This name was not known, rather G-d revealed it to the prophets. All the other names are taken from the honoring (titles) of humans and all of them have an explanation and definition, such as "Adon-ay" which is like "Adoney Yosef" (the masters of Yosef), and the judges are called "Elohim", etc. unlike the "Shem Hameforash" as the Kuzari extensively wrote about (Maamar 4 ot 1-3).
>
> Tov HaLevanon - His true name, as He is. What we are not capable of uttering in its true way (Translator: perhaps he means the 72 letter name uttered by the Kohen Gadol on Yom Kipur)

But as for His glorious essence and His true nature - there is no picture or likeness that we can grasp in our minds. Therefore, His Name is frequently changed in the Torah and likewise in the books of the prophets.

Because we cannot understand anything about Him except for His Name and that He exists. His glorious Name is also associated with heaven and earth and the Spirits, as Abraham said: "And I will make you swear by the L-ord, the G-d of heaven and the G-d of the earth" (Gen. 24:3), and Yonah said: "I fear the L-ord, the G-d of heaven" (1:9), and Moshe said: "the G-d of the spirit of all flesh" (Numbers 27:16). And the verse proclaims: "Behold, I am the L-ord, the G-d of all flesh" (Yirmiya 32:27).

> (*Tov Halevanon*: (His Name is changed in the Torah) such as the name "Yud-Hey-Vuv-Hey" which teaches that He was, is, and always will be. Or the name "Adon-ay" which teaches that He is master over the creations, or the name "Elo-him" - that He is powerful and all-capable, or the name "Sha-day" -

that He is "meshaded" the marachos. The verse adds "of heaven and earth" to teach that we do not completely understand His true Name but rather we see Him according to what we understand through His existence and deeds)

The reason for this is that He is known to us in the way possible through the traditions of our forefathers from whom we have inherited the knowledge of His ways, as written "For I have known him (Abraham), to the end that he may command his children and his household after him, that they may keep the way of the L-ord, to do righteousness and justice" (Gen. 18:19).

Perhaps, G-d revealed Himself to them because they were the only ones in their generation who took on to serve Him since the people of their generation worshipped other "gods" (idols, sun, moon, money, etc.)

Similarly we will explain for His being called (in scripture) "the G-d of the Hebrews" (Ex. 3:18), "the G-d of Yisrael" (Gen. 33:20), as the verse says "not like these is the portion of Yaakov for He is the Creator of all" (Yirmiya 10:16).

(*Pas Lechem*: i.e. the verse has called G-d "the portion of Yaakov", also for this reason - since G-d chose Yaakov for His portion, namely, to perform His service)

And David said: "O L-ord, the portion of mine inheritance and of my cup" (Ps. 16:5). And if we were able to grasp His true nature, He would not be known to us through other things.

(*Tov Halevanon*: His Divinity would not be a term described through our forefathers, heaven and earth, or "spirit of all flesh".)

Since it is not possible for our intellects to grasp His true nature, when referring to His glorious essence the scripture describes Him as the G-d of the choicest of His creations, rational or otherwise. Therefore, when Moshe Rabeinu asked G-d "when the Israelites ask me what is His name, what should I answer them?", G-d answered him: "so shall you say to the descendants of Israel: 'Ehe-ye' sent me to you'". And since G-d knew that the Israelites would not understand the true nature of this name (Ehe-ye), He added an explanation and said: "thus should you say to the Israelites: "The L-ord, the G-d of your forefathers, the G-d of Abraham, the G-d of Isaac, and the G-d of Jacob sent me to you, this... (Ex. 3:15)".

G-d's intent (to Moshe) in this was that if the people did not understand these words and their implications through intellectual reason, then tell them that I am known by them through the tradition they received from their ancestors. The Creator did not establish any other way to know Him except through these two ways, namely, (1) that which intellectual reason testifies through the evidence of His deeds which are visible in His creations, (2) and that of ancestral tradition, as scripture says: "Which wise men have told from their fathers, and have not hid it" (Iyov 15:18).

And since our perception of all existing things is through one of three ways:
1. Physical perception, such as through sight, hearing, taste, smell, or touch.
2. Through our reason, by which the existence of something is demonstrated from its indications and effects, until the reality of its existence and nature are established to us as if we perceived it with our physical senses.

> (*Marpe Lenefesh*: see end of chapter 6, the example of finding a letter with orderly style and uniform handwriting which demonstrates that there exists a man who knows how to write who wrote this letter, even though we never saw him. Hence, the handwriting is proof on him as if we saw him with our senses. So too for other similar things.)

This is called in the book of proverbs "understanding and intellectual discipline" (Mishlei 1:2-3).

> (*Manoach Halevavos*: The habitual practice, that a man habituates himself to understand the ways of proofs, and the premises and logical relationships to understand the intellectual things. And since a man must discipline himself for some time to understand the depth of the things difficult for him, until he is habituated in them - therefore it is called "intellectual discipline")

3. True reports and reliable tradition.

Since it is not possible for us to perceive the Creator through our senses, we can only know Him through true reports or from proofs on Him based on the evidence of His deeds.

> (*Marpe Lenefesh*: - the Kuzari wrote (Maamar 1 Ot 25): "it is the duty of the entire congregation of Israel to believe all that is written in the Torah, since it has been clarified to them that great assembly (at Mount Sinai) with their own eyes, and afterwards the ensuing tradition which is considered as if one saw it with his own eyes.

And since the proofs drawn from the evidence of His deeds in the creations are established and greatly numerous, therefore the attributes ascribed to Him because of them are also numerous.

The saints and the prophets described His attributes in different ways. Moshe Rabeinu said "The Rock, His work is perfect, for all His ways are justice" (Deut. 32:4), and he also said: "He is G-d of gods, and L-ord of lords, the great G-d, the mighty, and the awesome" (Deut. 10:17), and also "He exacts justice for the fatherless and the widow" (Deut. 10:18). And G-d Himself described His own attributes as written: "And the L-ord passed by before him, and proclaimed: 'The L-ord, the L-ord, G-d, merciful and gracious, long-suffering, and abundant in goodness and truth, keeping mercy unto the thousandth generation, forgiving iniquity and transgression and sin, etc.'" (Ex. 34:6).

> (*Tov Halevanon*: All of these different attributes is because we are not capable of reaching even the tiniest part of praise that is befitting to Him.
>
> *Marpe Lenefesh*: We are not capable of understanding even one of His praises. For example, when we praise Him with the praise "righteous judge", "merciful", "gracious", - who is capable of knowing or making known how He is a righteous judge? Sometimes He decrees on this man poverty, destitution, and sufferings, and everything was just, while other times such a person lacks no good. Likewise for merciful and gracious or the like. Therefore any praise we say of Him due to the signs of His wisdom and deeds is not even a drop in the ocean compared to what is befitting Him.)

(That G-d possesses) these attributes we see from the evidence of His deeds towards His creations and also from the wisdom and power which His deeds reflect. And if we investigate this matter with our intellect and understanding, we will fail to grasp the smallest of the smallest of part of His attributes, as David said: "Many, O L-ord my G-d, are Your wonderful works which You have done, and Your thoughts which are toward us..." (Ps. 40:6), and "Who can utter the mighty acts of the L-ord? who can show forth all his praise?" (Ps. 106:2), and "And blessed be Your glorious name, which is exalted above all blessing and praise" (Nehemiah 9:5). And the Sages said in the Talmud (Berachos 33b):

A certain person led the prayer service before Rabbi Chanina and said: "the great, the mighty, the awesome, the powerful, the glorious, the potent, the feared, the strong, the powerful, the certain, and the esteemed G-d!". R' Chanina waited until he finished. When he finished, R' Chanina said to him: "did you complete all the praises of your Master? What need is there for all of this? even us, these three praises that we say (in the daily prayers), if not for the fact that Moshe Rabeinu said it in the Torah (Deut. 10:17), and the men of the great assembly came and established it in prayer, we wouldn't be able to say them! And you say all these praises and continue? It is analogous to a king of flesh and blood who had thousands upon thousands of golden coins, and they would praise him for possessing silver coins, isn't this a disgrace to him"?

And "to You silence is praise" (Ps. 65:2), to which our teachers said: "the best potion is silence, the more you praise a flawless pearl, the more you depreciate it" (Megila 18a).

Therefore, you should exert your mind until you know the Creator through the evidences of His works and not strive to know Him in His glorious essence. For He is exceedingly close to you from the side of His deeds but infinitely remote in any representation of His essence or comparison with it. As already stated, we will never be able to find Him in this way. When you arrive at the stage where you abandon (trying to find Him) through your thoughts and senses because He cannot be grasped in this way, and you instead find Him in the evidence of His deeds, as though He were inseparable from you - this is the pinnacle of knowledge of Him which the prophet exhorts us on in saying "Know therefore this day, and consider it in your heart, that the L-ord He is G-d in heaven above, and upon the earth beneath: there is none else" (Deut. 4:39).

One of the Sages said: "the more one increases knowledge of the Creator, the more one is awe-struck with regard to His nature" (realizes how little he understands of Him - *TL*).

Others said: "the truly wise person in the knowledge of G-d realizes his ignorance regarding His glorious essence while the ignorant person thinks that he understands G-d's glorious essence." (his understanding of G-d is in the way of materializing or through form or likeness - *TL*).

One of the Sages was asked on the Creator: "what is He?". He answered: "One G-d". The asker then asked: "What is He like?". He answered "A great King". He then asked: "Where is He?" He answered: "in the mind".

> *Tov Halevanon*: i.e. the mind's eye, He cannot be found in any place. Only through reason we know His existence, that at least He exists

The asker: "I did not ask you on this"

> *Tov Halevanon*: i.e. I did not mean to ask on existence in the mind, namely, intellectually where is He. Rather I meant, concretely - where is He in space?

The sage answered: "You asked me on attributes which apply to created things, not to the Creator. And the attributes which can be ascribed to the Creator, I replied to you, (and even these (i.e. one G-d, great King, that He dwells secretly in the hidden realm of intellect, are not befitting Him and - *ML*) the reason we ascribe them to Him is) because otherwise it would be impossible for us to know Him.

It is said of one of the Sages who would say in his prayer: "My G-d, where can I find You, yet where can I not find You. You are hidden and invisible yet everything is filled with You, similar to the verse "Do I not fill heaven and earth says the L-ord" (Yirmiya 23:24).

> *Tov Halevanon*: He is not localized in any place whatsoever,

but from the side of spiritual life force of everything created, it is clear to us that nothing is devoid of Him.

The pinnacle of knowing Him is to reach the stage where you admit and believe that you are completely ignorant of the truth of His glorious essence.

> *Pas Lechem*: that you admit this before Him, and believe in your heart that this is truly so, and not like one who praises flesh and blood who says praises but His heart does not believe in them.

If you form in your mind a picture or representation of the Creator, strive to investigate His Being.

> *Tov Halevanon*: through the proofs which demonstrate that the Creator is exalted above any likeness or form and that they are merely Mikre (incidental properties) of His creations.

Then you will clarify His existence.

> *Pas Lechem*: you will clarify that His existence is hidden and beyond any comparison.

And you will reject any type of likeness of Him, until you will find Him only through the way of reasoning.

> (*Pas Lechem*: "way of reasoning" - this refers to His deeds which are proofs to us of His existence.

The analogy of this:
We realize the truth of existence of the soul without perceiving of it any form or likeness, or appearance or smell, even though its effects are visible and its acts are recognizable in us.

> *Tov Halevanon*: The soul does not occupy any "place", even though it fills the body, it has no physical place. And that which the Sages say that the soul dwells in the heart or the brain, this only refers to the beginning of its influence. But certainly it does not dwell there in space..

Likewise the intellect whose effects and signs are evident and noticeable, yet the intellect has no form or likeness, nor can we compare it in our thoughts.

> *Marpe Lenefesh*: - through the intellect we think and understand things, yet we don't understand what it is.

And all the more so - the Creator of everything, which there is none like Him. And a philosopher said: "if our efforts to fully know the soul are vain, all the more so for the matter of the Creator".

Since we have reached until here in our discussion, it is not necessary to proceed further.

> (*Marpe Lenefesh*: - Likewise the Kuzari wrote several times - that distant proofs and logical explanations cause a man to stray and bring him to apikorsut (heresy), and he extensively wrote on this throughout his just book. And his opinion throughout the book is that a man should be simple with G-d (Deut. 18:13) without investigations and proofs, see there)

The reason being, that it is our duty to be in fear and awe, and to guard from it, as some of the Sages said: "that which is beyond you, do not expound, that which is hidden from you, do not investigate. That which is permitted to you - contemplate. Do not have any business with hidden things" (Ben Sira in Megila 13a).

And our Sages said: "whoever is not concerned for the honor of his Creator it is better for him had he not been created" (Chagiga 11b). And they expounded on the verse "Shall it be told him that I speak? if a man speaks, surely he shall be swallowed up" (Iyov 37:20) - Whoever comes to speak the might of G-d will be destroyed (Talmud Yerushalmi Berachos 9a). And the verse says: "And he struck the men of Beth Shemesh, because they had looked into the ark of the L-ord" (Shmuel 6:19) (who stared at it with coarse hearts, without due awe- PL), and "It is the glory of G-d to conceal a thing" (Mishlei 25:2), which means to conceal His secret from men who are not wise (since due to their weak intellect there will remain nothing left for them to believe in - *TL*), and "the secret of G-d is with them that fear Him" (Ps. 25:14).

Furthermore regarding the physical senses we mentioned and the mental faculties, namely, memory, thought, imagination, counsel/will, recognition, which all refer to one power, namely, the mind which gives them the ability to apprehend things.

THE PHYSICAL SENSES

Each one of the (physical) senses has a distinct ability to perceive certain types of sensations which the other senses lack. For example, form and color can only be perceived by the sense of sight. Voices and music can only be perceived by the sense of hearing. Scent and various odors - only by the sense of smell. Various tastable things - only by the sense of taste. Hot and cold and many matters of quality - by the sense of touch.

Each sense has a power to perceive its relevant sensation to a definite extent, beyond which it is incapable of perceiving further. For example, sight has the ability to perceive something close by, and the further away one goes, the weaker its ability to apprehend it, until eventually it ceases to apprehend it completely. Likewise for the sense of hearing, and also for the other senses.

And it is impossible to grasp a sensation without the appropriate sense designated for it. One who strives to grasp it with a different sense will fail to accomplish his desire. For example, one who strives to grasp a melody with the sense of sight or visible things with the sense of smell or taste with the sense of touch - he will not be able to find them or grasp them, despite that they exist, because one is trying to perceive them without the limbs designated for perceiving these sensations.

Likewise we will say for the mental faculties we mentioned. Each one of them has a distinct power to perceive a specific thing which the others cannot, and a limit to which it can grasp no further, as we mentioned for the physical senses.

Likewise we will say for the mind (in total) which grasps intellectual things by itself or through proofs. For things that are close to it, it will grasp its truth directly through itself, while for things which are remote and hidden, it will grasp it through building proofs which point to it.

And since the Creator is infinitely remote and hidden for us from the side of His glorious essence, the intellect can grasp only that He exists. (since neither the physical nor the mental senses have any path or approach to build any proofs on Him - *TL*)

And if it strives to grasp His glorious essence or to imagine Him - even His existence will be hidden to it (and one will think that He does not exist - *TL*), because it strove to grasp something beyond its ability, as we mentioned for trying to grasp a sensation with the wrong sense.

Therefore, we must seek the existence of G-d through the evidence of His deeds in the creations - and these will be proofs on Him for us. And when His existence is established for us in this way, we must then cease and not seek to liken Him in our thoughts or to try to represent or figure Him in our imagination, or attempt to apprehend His glorious essence. For, if we do this, thinking we will understand Him more closely - even the realization of His existence will disappear from us, because anything we imagine in our minds will be other than Him. And scripture says: "Have you found honey? eat only as much as is sufficient for you, lest you be filled with it, and vomit it" (Mishlei 25:16).

> (*Tov Halevanon*: This verse is an analogy on the study of the hidden, that one should learn or examine only until the limit he is capable of grasping, since otherwise he will vomit even that which he learned and no emuna (faith) will be left in him.)

I saw fitting to try to bring the matter close to you using two illustrations.

The First of the two will demonstrate that each physical sense perceives its class of sensations and then it reaches its limit whereby the next physical sense picks up where it left off. And afterwards, it will also reach its limit and the next sense will start, and so on for all the senses. When they all reach their limit of perception, the intellect will then start to perceive what is in its power to apprehend. This will be demonstrated by means of one object.

Imagine that a stone was thrown far away. It makes a whistling/crashing noise and strikes a man. The man perceived with his sense of sight the appearance of the stone and its form. Then he perceives with his sense of hearing the whistling/crashing noise, then he perceives with his sense of touch the coldness and hardness of it. Afterwards, the physical senses cease to apprehend any more of the stone. Then the intellect perceives that the stone must have had a thrower who threw it, since it is clear to it that the stone did not move from its place by itself.

That which is normally perceived through the physical senses cannot be apprehended by the intellect without the physical senses. And all the more so, that which is normally perceived by the intellect cannot be perceived by the physical senses.

> *Marpe Lenefesh*: He is now giving a reason why the intellect did not perceive the matter from beginning to end. He says: it is impossible for the intellect to perceive that which is perceived by the physical senses, namely, the noise and the touch. If he did not see the rock, hear the noise, or feel the strike, the intellect would not have known whether or not there was any stone which produced a noise or struck. Likewise for other similar things. From there he will make a kal v'chomer (major to minor logical inference) - if the intellect cannot perceive that which is normally perceived with physical senses, all the more so that it is impossible for the physical senses to perceive what is normally perceived by the intellect (since the intellect is on a higher plane.

The second illustration will demonstrate that for spiritual matters, once we are convinced of their existence, it is not proper to investigate their nature because this approach only ruins our intellect. This is like one who tries to understand the sun from observing its light, radiance, shine, and its power to dissipate darkness. If he accepts its existence, he will benefit from it, use its light, and attain all that he seeks from it (and will know for certain that the sun exists - TL). But one who strives to study its roundness and focuses his eyes to stare at it - his eyes will dim and (eventually) their sight will be lost and he will not benefit from the sun. (not even from its light - TL).

The same thing will happen to us. If we study the existence of the Creator from the evidence of His signs in the creations, the wisdom manifested in them, His power shown in all His creations - we will think and we will understand His nature. Then our minds will be illuminated with knowledge of Him and we will attain all that is possible for us to attain, as written "I am the L-ord your G-d who teaches you for your benefit, who leads you by the way that you should go" (Isaiah 48:17).

But if we exert our minds to understand the matter of His glorious essence, and to try to liken or represent Him in our minds - we will ruin/diminish our intellect and understanding, and we will not grasp even what was known to us, as would happen to our eyes if we stared at the sun. We must be careful in this matter, and remember it when we investigate on the matter of the existence of G-d.

> (*Marpe Lenefesh*: - As we find recorded in books, that most of the early philosophers became insane. And we see even in our generation - those groups which go after their opinions and investigations, either they became crazy or they go out to evil ways... Perhaps this explains: "Ben Zoma looked and was damaged, and Acher went out to evil ways" (Chagiga 14b regarding the 4 great Sages who entered Paradise upstairs using holy names). One must be careful and guard to not represent G-d with any likeness or form, G-d forbid. We must remember this in our investigations in this gate when examining the matter of the existence of the Creator. We must also guard to not represent Him or ascribe to Him any kind of physical form. Likewise, the Moray (Rambam's Guide for the Perplexed Part 1 ch.35) wrote: "just like it is necessary for the masses to realize and the young ones to be taught that G-d is one, and that one must not serve other than Him. So too, it is necessary to educate them in this in the way of tradition that G-d does not have a body and that there is absolutely no comparison in any way whatsoever between Him and His creations." He then ends off with "even though they don't understand the reasons for the matter and don't know the logical proofs which establish the matter in the mind, just like you are not obligated to teach him by proofs that G-d exists. Rather, let them accept everything in the way of tradition, and afterwards when they grow, the matter will be explained to them stage by stage according to their intellectual ability", see there for more details)

Likewise, we must be careful regarding His attributes, whether those which describe His glorious essence or those the prophets ascribe to Him - not to take them literally or according to what would seem in a physical sense.

> (*Pas Lechem*: In scripture there are verses with expressions
> of His glorious essence which are said in first person form
> such as "See now that I, I am He, and there is no god with
> Me" (Deut. 32:39), while other expressions which the
> prophets speak in third person)

Rather, we must know clearly that they are in a metaphorical and
incidental sense according to what we are capable of grasping with
our powers of recognition, understanding, and intellect, due to our
crucial need to know Him and His loftiness. But He is infinitely
greater and loftier above all of this, and like the verse says "Blessed
be Your glorious Name, that is exalted above all blessing and
praise" (Nehemiah 9:5).

One of the philosophers said: "He whose mind is too weak to
understand the matter of divesting (he cannot strip off the physical
from the terms which connote abstract spiritual matters - *ML*), he
holds fast to the terms in the Divinely given scriptures, and does not
realize that the terms in scripture are adapted to the intelligence of
those to whom they were addressed, not according to (the
intelligence) of the One who addressed them. Rather they are like
the whistling call to a herd of cattle at the time of water drinking,
which brings them to drink far more effectively than clear and
accurate words."

When you master this level of the Unity in your intellect and
understanding, devote your soul to the Creator, strive to grasp His
existence from (observing) His wisdom, His power, His grace, His
mercy, and His abundant providence over His creations. Become
pleasing to Him by doing His will. Then you will be among the
seekers of G-d (and it is written: "those who seek G-d will
understand all" (Mishlei 28:5) - *ML*), and then you will receive from
Him the help and strength to understand Him, and to know His true
nature, as David said: "The secret of the L-ord is with them that fear
Him; and He will show them His covenant" (Ps. 25:14). I will clarify
for you some illustrations in the second gate of this book. When you
practice them, and go in their path, the matter will be easier for you
with G-d's help.

THINGS DETRIMENTAL

The things detrimental to the (wholehearted acceptance of G-d's) unity are numerous. Among them, to association of other beings with the Creator. This occurs in several ways.

Among them, believing in multiple gods, worshipping forms, the sun, moon, constellations, fire, plants, animals.

> (Manoach Halevavos - That one serves them, by associating them with G-d, even though one knows that the stars and idols are themselves not divine, and intends only to draw down their spiritual powers, and even though one thinks this will be pleasing to G-d that one serves His creations)

Among them, ascribing physicality to the Creator, while understanding the true intent of scripture.

Among them, hidden association, namely trying to find favor with other people with regard to religious matters. This occurs in several ways. I will clarify them in the fifth gate of this book, with G-d's help.

> (*Marpe Lenefesh*: - "hidden" in that other people do not know his intent, that he associates something else with G-d, namely that he serves G-d with fraudulent intent, but "visibly" he appears as if he is serving G-d alone...)

Among them, turning (excessively) to the physical pleasures. This is subtle association - that a man associates the service of his lusts with the service of the Creator. And the verse says: "There shall not be in you a strange god", to which our Rabbis expound: "what is the 'strange god' which is in the body of a man? - This is the evil inclination" (Talmud Shabbos 105b).

> (*Marpe Lenefesh*: - When a man turns to the physical pleasures, he will not stop nor rest day and night, and all of his aspirations will be to fulfill his desires. And all of his acts are not l'shem shamayim (for G-d), because he will always look first - whether he will receive benefit from it. If yes, then he will do it. But if not, he will drop it all)

Perhaps the simple and foolish person, when he reads this book and considers what we wrote in this gate will say to himself: "will the matter of unity of G-d be unknown to anyone who reads even one page of the Torah whereby this author needs to stir us and instruct us it?"

I will answer this as the wise man answered: "Answer a fool according to his folly" (Mishlei 26:5). For one who asks this is too weak of understanding to grasp the extent of a universal topic which is addressed to different classes of people. Such a universal topic is grasped differently depending on whether the person understood much of it or little of it, and whether he is of strong intellect or of weak intellect.

> (*Tov Halevanon*: so too, for one who claims to have understood the matter of unity by learning one page this is because his understanding is weak and he does not benefit from the matters of the Unity hinted at in the Torah. His benefit is like the benefit of a blind man from the light of the sun, as will be explained.)

The analogy to this - the benefit of the light of the sun which is universal to all men. We find this benefit divides into three classes: The first class: Those whose eyes are healthy and free from all diseases. They benefit from the sun, use its light, and attain all types of benefit from it.

The second class: The totally blind, whose eyesight is completely lost. The light of the sun does not damage nor benefit them. Their benefit from it is through other people (who guide them).

The third class: People whose eyes are too weak to tolerate the light of the sun, and the sun's light will damage them if they don't avoid it. If they hasten to heal their eyes with medications, potions, and therapeutic diets, and at the same time are careful not to expose their eyes to the light of the sun - it is possible that they will become healthy and they will benefit from the sun which was previously damaging to them. But if they delay healing their eyes, they will quickly lose their eyesight completely and belong to the class of the totally blind.

Similarly, the classes of understanding G-d's unity taught in the Torah divides into three classes. The matter is taught to all rational beings, just like the light of the sun is available to all seeing beings.

The first class: Men of clear intellect and pure understanding.

The second class: Men whose intellect is completely too weak to understand anything of what is written in the Torah.

The third class: Men whose intellect is too weak to grasp what the first class is able to grasp but they have sufficient intelligence to comprehend most of the near and easy matters.

The first class, namely, the men of complete intellect, free from all detriment. When they put to heart to understand what they encountered in the Torah on the matter of the Unity, they will understand it, and its matter will enter their heart through their powerful understanding and pure intellect. They are of those who don't need this book, except to remind them of what has escaped their attention.

> (*Marpe Lenefesh*: - Certainly they don't need to plumb in-depth to bring proofs on the Unity of G-d, since none of this is hidden to them due to their powerful intellect and understanding. Also, every man, especially those who study the Torah, need that there should be before them a "book of remembrance" of mussar and yira, especially this book, so that one can rebuke and reprimand himself always from within the book, lest and perhaps one goes out from the bounds of the service of G-d, without realizing. Therefore it is necessary to consider and examine one's acts always. Because the yetzer (evil inclination) is close by, and does not leave a person who does any good thing until he has enticed him to abandon it, like the author wrote in the fifth gate...as the maggid (angel) prescribed to the Beis Yosef (to study daily from the Chovos Halevavos to subjugate the yetzer)...and in my book "HaZechiros", I elaborated a bit also from other early books on the greatness of the obligation on every Jew to always toil in books of yira and mussar, and especially Torah scholars, since the greater a man, the greater is his yetzer.)

The second class do not know G-d's Torah, all the more so the matter of Unity in it. They hear its teaching but do not comprehend its matter. They will have neither benefit nor damage from this book.

The third class who understand the matter of the Unity mentioned in G-d's Torah with some understanding, but they don't have the intellectual power to understand its matter and realize its true meaning. If a teacher instructs them and makes them understand its matter through the way of true proofs and sound intellectual reasoning - its meaning will become clear to them, and its secret will be revealed to them, and they will reach the level of the first class.

But if they shirk from investigating and are lazy in examining in that which will strengthen their understanding and sharpen their intellect - they will sink to the level of the foolish.

To those of this class, this book will be of great and comprehensive benefit, because they are capable of investigating. It will benefit them just like potions benefit those with weak eyesight, who hope to be healed by their application.

Scripture already compared the foolish man - to a blind man, wisdom - to light, and foolishness - to darkness, in saying: "Then I saw that wisdom excels folly, as far as light excels darkness" (Eccles. 2:13), and "The wise man's eyes are in his head; but the fool walks in darkness" (Eccles. 2:14), and "Hear, you deaf; and look, you blind, that you may see" (Isaiah 42:18).

> (*Pas Lechem*: The wise man is he who sees the future consequences. When he stands at the beginning of a matter, he contemplates and thinks about what will happen at the end of it. Unlike the fool, who is like one who walks in darkness who does not see what is ahead of him)

And they compared wisdom and mussar - to a tree of life (which a man eats from and lives forever - *PL*), as written: "It is a tree of life to them that lay hold upon it" (Mishlei 3:18), and "For they are life unto those that find them" (Mishlei 4:22).

> (*Tov Halevanon*: Not only does wisdom benefit to heal the eyes of the intellect but rather it is an elixir of life to the entire body and the soul)

May the Almighty teach us the way to the knowledge Him, direct us to His service, and bestow on us His grace, in His mercy and compassion. Amen.

*** TRANSLATOR'S SUMMARY ***

The following is a brief summary of the logical proof of the existence of G-d from the Shaar Yichud according to the translator's limited understanding. Note that it is impossible to arrive at a water-tight mathematical type proof as the author wrote in his introduction to this book:

> I propose to take the most direct (easiest) method of arousing, teaching, and instructing, using language clear, direct, and familiar, so that my words will be more easily understood. I will refrain from deep language, unusual terms, and the arguments in the way of *"defeat"* (nitzuach), which the logicians call in arabic *"Algidal"*, and likewise for remote inquiries which cannot be resolved in this work, for I only brought such arguments as are satisfactory and convincing according to the methods proper to the science of theology.
>
> As the philosopher said "it is not proper to seek of every inquiry a conclusion in the way of mofet (irrefutable proof), since not every topic in rational inquiry can be demonstrated to this extent. Likewise, we should not be satisfied in the science of nature with the method of 'sufficient' (since a full "raya" proof can be achieved there through experiment). Nor in the science of theology should we strive to apprehend with the senses or draw comparisons with physical phenomena."
>
> > (*Tov Halevanon commentary*: *"defeat"* (nitzuach) - It is known that the science of logic divides into three methods nitzuach (defeat), raya (proof), and mofet (definitive proof). Nitzuach (defeat) is when one cannot decide on either of the two views definitively, only that one view has more and stronger questions and claims which can be raised against it than the other view. The view which has fewer and weaker questions against it will prevail over the other view, and it is proper to follow that view even though it may also have some questions which can be raised. The "proof" (raya) is where one view has many questions and claims which can be raised against it while the other view has no claims against it.

Certainly, it is proper to uphold it. This is better than nitzuach (defeat). Because here there are no claims and questions against it from the aspect of rational inquiry, but nevertheless, perhaps his inquiry was somehow flawed [for example, due to lacking certain information]. The "mofet" (definitive proof) is that which is impossible to refute, in almost any way whatsoever, similar to the miracles of the prophets which were openly visible to the senses [at that time]. Behold, science is divided into three divisions: theology, nature, mathematics. It is known that for most of the science of theology, it is impossible to bring a "raya" (proof), and all the more so, a mofet (definitive proof).

For due to the enormous depth and awesomeness of this science, and the limitations of human intellect, it is almost impossible to establish a clear view which is without any doubts. But they can be clarified in the way of Nitzuach (defeat), and a few of its topics through "raya" (proof) which are close to being mofet (definitive proof). For the science of nature, on the other hand, which is not as deep, one can explain much of it in the way of raya (proof), and some even from mofet (definitive proof). But the science of limudit which is the science of mathematics and geometry, all of its matters are clarified through mofet (definitive proof). This is what the author wrote that not all rational inquiry is found as mofet (definitive proof), but as nitzuach (defeat) or rayah (proof).)

(*Pas Lechem commentary*: for it is impossible to explain things in theology using our physical senses or to explain it through a familiar analogy, because it is exalted above and beyond all senses and comparison. It has no connection whatsoever with these things.)

Let us begin. By understanding the (theological) proof that G-d must exist, we will automatically get an introduction to G-d. Although it is impossible for us to understand Him directly nevertheless we can at least understand to some small extent what He is not.

Now, the logical proof of G-d is based on three premises
1. A thing cannot make itself.
2. causal chains cannot be infinite in number.
3. Anything composite is not eternally existing.

Regarding the first premise: It is self-evident that something which is totally non-existent cannot do anything. And if it does something, then it is already existing.

If you ask, physicists find particles (quantum fluctuations) which appear and disappear in empty space. Answer: as explained in chapter 5, the particles do not pop out of nowhere. They are consequences and properties of a pre-existing space-time medium governed by pre-existing laws of quantum mechanics. Thus, there are not at all coming from absolutely nothing. See there for more.

Regarding the second premise, causal chains cannot be infinite in number. This means you cannot explain the existence of an egg by saying there is an infinite regress of chicken-egg, chicken-egg, and so on, endlessly.

Another analogy, if we have a room of parallel mirrors with infinite reflections of a human face. You can't reasonably explain the existence of the faces in the mirror by saying there is no source face and they are all just reflections of each other. In reality, there must exist a source, a real human face otherwise nothing would be reflected in the mirrors.

Hence according to these two premises, to explain the effect of the existence of the universe requires us to conclude that something exists which is eternal (without beginning). Now, the question is what can be eternal?

The third premise states that anything composite cannot be eternal (without beginning). The eternal by definition cannot have anything preceding it. So for example, "dough" needs flour and water to exist, hence "dough" cannot be eternal since its existence depends on the pre-existence of flour and water.

What about something like an electron or a photon or even spacetime? These things are composite in a subtler sense. They are composites of themselves and their "boundaries/limitations /properties". For example, an electron has position, spin, charge, mass, momentum, energy, etc. Therefore it is a composite of itself and whatever boundaries, limitations or properties were set on it. Hence it is a composite of two matters - 1) its own existence and 2) from the aspect of that which it must have a cause which set its boundaries/properties/limitations. i.e., it has to be a result of a previous "something" that either "made" it or "shaped" it or "defined" it - something which CAUSED its borders/properties, etc. to be what they are.

For example, a video game has certain characters, each one having certain properties, abilities, or position on the screen, etc. These things must have been set by a computer programmer. They cannot just exist eternally, without beginning.

Hence, the only thing that can be Eternal (without beginning) is that which has no properties or limitations in any way. It is completely infinite and boundless in all respects. It has no parts or boundaries. This is a completely different "kind" of existence than anything we are familiar with. Anything else which has some sort of limitation or property cannot be eternal.

This automatically rules out anything physical or more than one Eternal (since then each supposed Eternal would be limited in some sense and therefore automatically could not be eternal) and leaves only the One G-d. He is One in an absolute sense.

Obviously, we have no way whatsoever of comprehending such an infinite existence, but we can know for sure that the Eternal must exist otherwise we would not be here. By studying the world with this outlook, we can learn about the Eternal.

Once this is clear, it follows that prophecy is necessary for Him to tell us what this is all about and this leads us to the first and foremost book on prophecy - the torah. (see torah authenticity at dafyomireview.com/430 for much more on this).

Here's a quote from the Pas Lechem commentary in ch.7 which

summarizes this.

> He began with the title: "powerful" because according to our understanding, He existed before everything, since immediately after we grasp that there exists a Creator who created the world from nothing, we will immediately recognize His power, namely, the act of creating something from nothing...After this, when we reflect on the details of creation, and we study them and their parts - we will see signs of His wisdom and we will know that He is wise. Afterwards, we contemplate His providence in governing the world, we will know that He is living and among us always. Understand that all of these descriptions are obligatory and follow one after the other, with the creation of the world as their first source.

To summarize, G-d is the "muchrach hametziut" (the necessary existence), and that which is the necessary existence IS the Existence itself (Rabbi Moshe Shapiro).

שכלל אותם ככלול אור השמש לכל בעלי העינים כאשר זכרנו ומתחלקת הבנתם לשלשה חלקים.

האחד מהם אנשי השכל הצלול והתכונות הזכות.

והחלק השני בני אדם ששכלם חלש מהבין מה שיש בספר התורה לגמרי.

והחלק השלישי בני אדם שקצר שכלם מהשיג כמו הכת הראשונה אך יש בהם כח להכיר הענינים הקרובים הקלים.

והכת הראשונה שהם אנשי השכל השלם הנמלט מכל פגע כשהם משימים אל לבם מה שהגיע אליהם בספר התורה יבינו אותם ויכנס ענינו בלבם בכח הבנתם מכוח שכלם ואלה הם שאינם צריכים אל הספר הזה אלא להזכירם דבר שהתעלמו ממנו.

אך הכת השניה אינה יודעת ספר תורת אלהים כל שכן היחוד אשר בו והם שומעים את שמעו ואינם מבינים ענינו אין להם תועלת בספרי זה כלל.

והכת השלישית שמבינים היחוד אשר בספר תורת אלהים קצת הבנה ואין בכח הכרתם להבין ענינו ולעמוד על אמתתו אם יורם אותו מורה וביבנם ענינו על דרך המופתים האמתיים והראיות השכליות יתברר להם ענינו ויגלה להם סודו ויגיעו בכת הראשונה.

ואם יתעלמו מחקור ויתרשלו מעיין במה שיחזק הכרתם וילטוש שכלם, ירדו אל מדרגת הפתאים.

וספרי זה מועיל לכת הזאת תועלת גדולה וכוללת מפני שיכולים לחקור ויהיה להם הספר הזה ככחלים המועילים לבעלי העינים החלושות שמקוים הארוכה ברפאם אותם.

וכבר המשיל הספר האדם הכסיל בעור והחכמה באור והסכלות בחשך באמרו (קהלה ב) וראיתי אני שיש יתרון לחכמה מן הסכלות כיתרון האור מן החשך ואמר (שם) החכם עיניו בראשו והכסיל בחשך הולך ואמר (ישעיה מב) החרשים שמעו והעורים הביטו לראות.

והמשיל החכמה והמוסר בעץ החיים ככתוב (משלי ג) עץ חיים היא למחזיקים בה וגו' ואמר (שם ו) כי חיים הם למוצאיהם.

ואלהים יורנו דרך ידיעתו ויישירנו לעבודתו ויפיק לנו רצונו ברחמיו ובחמלתו, אמן: נשלם שער היחוד בעזרת האל האחד הקדמון:

השגחתו על ברואיו והתרצה אליו בעשות רצונו, אז תהיה ממבקשי ה' ואז תשיג ממנו העזר והאומץ להבינו ולדעת אמתת ענינו כמו שאמר דוד ע"ה (תהלים כה) סוד ה' ליראיו ובריתו להודיעם. ואני עתיד לבאר לך דמיונות בשער השני מן הספר הזה כשתתנהג בהם ותלך בנתיביהם יקל עליך הדבר בעזרת האל יתעלה.

אך מפסידות היחוד בלב שלם הרבה מהם לשתף הבורא והוא על כמה פנים.

מהם בהנחת הרבוי ומהם בעבודת הצורות ועבודת השמש והירח והמזלות.

ומהם השתוף הנעלם והוא החונף בעניני הדת לבני אדם. והוא על כמה ענינים אני עתיד לבאר אותם בשער החמישי מן הספר הזה בעזרת השם.

ומהם הנטיה אל תאות הגופות המגונות כי הוא שתוף נעלם שמשתתף האדם עם עבודת אלהיו עבודת תאותו והכתוב אומר (שם פא) לא יהיה בך אל זר ואמרו רז"ל איזהו אל זר שיש בגופו של אדם הוי אומר זה יצה"ר.

ושמא הכסיל הפתי כשיקרא הספר הזה ויעמוד על מה שזכרנו בשער הזה יאמר בלבו, היעלם ענין היחוד ממי שלמד דף אחד מן התורה עד שיעיד אותנו המחבר הזה עליו ויורנו אותו.

אומר בתשובתו, כמו שצוה החכם (משלי כז) ענה כסיל כאולתו וגו' כי האומר זה הכרתו חלושה להבין כלל הענינים הנאמרים על מינים נחלקים וקבולם מתחלק ברב ובמעט ובחזק ובחלש.

והדומה לזה תועלת אור השמש שכוללת כל בני האדם ומצאנו אותה מתחלקת לשלשה חלקים.

האחד מהם למי שעיניהם מאירות ונצלות מכל חלי שהם נהנים מן השמש ומשתמשים לאורה ומגיעים לכל הנאתם ממנה.

והחלק השני העורים אשר נעדר אור עיניהם לגמרי אין השמש מועילה אותם ולא מזקת אותם אבל תועלתם ממנה תהיה ע"י שליח.

והחלק השלישי בני אדם שנחלשו עיניהם מהשתמש בהם כנגד השמש והשמש מזקת אותם אם לא יסתירום מאורה שאם ימהרו לרפא עיניהם בכחלים וברטיות ובתקון מאכלם עם שמירת עיניהם מהשתמש בהם לאור השמש. אפשר שיגיעו אל הבריאות ויהנו בשמש שהיתה מזקת אליהם. ואם יתעכבו לרפא עיניהם יגיעו אל כת העורים במהרה ויעדר מאור עינם לגמרי.

ועל הדמיון הזה יתחלק ענין היחוד הנכתב בספר התורה לקהלת המדברים אחר

קרירותה וקשיותה ואחר עמדו החושים הגשמיים ולא השיגו מענין האבן יותר מזה ואחר כך השיג השכל כי יש לאבן משליך השליכה מפני שהתברר כי האבן לא נדה ממקומה מאליה.

כי מה שדרכו שיושג בחושים הגשמיים ימנע מהשכל להשיגו בבלעדיהם כ"ש שימנע מהחושים הגשמיים מה שדרכו שיושג בשכל בלבד. וכיון שנמנע משכלנו להשיג הוית עצם כבוד הבורא יתברך איך יהיה לנו רשות להמשילו או להגבילו ולדמותו לשום דבר ממושגי חושינו הגשמיים וזה דבר נמנע.

והדמיון השני יורך כי העניניים הרוחניים כאשר נעמוד על ברור מציאותם אין מן הזריזות לדקדק בהם ולחקור על גופם כי זה מפסיד את שכלנו. וזה כמי שטרח להשיג השמש מצד אורה וניצוצה וזריחתה ודוחק האופל ממנה יעמוד על מציאותה ונהנה ממנה ומשתמש לאורה ומגיע אל הענין המבוקש ממנה. ומי שיטרח למצאה מצד עגולה וכוון בעיניו להביט אל עין השמש תכהינה עיניו ויעדר אורם ולא יהנה מהשמש.

וכן יקרנו כשנשיג מציאות הבורא יתעלה מצד אותותיו וחכמתו בהם ויכלתו בכל בראיו נשכיל ונבין ענינו אז יאור שכלנו בידיעתו ונשיג כל מה שיש בכח שכלנו להשיגו כמ"ש (ישעיה מח) אני ה' אלהיך מלמדך להועיל מדריכך בדרך תלך.

ואם נטריח שכלנו להשיג ענין עצם כבודו ולדמותו ולהמשילו במחשבותינו נפקד שכלנו והכרתנו ולא נשיג בהם שום דבר מן הידוע לנו כמו שיקרה לנו בהביטנו אל עין השמש. וצריכים אנו להזהר בענין הזה ולזכרו בחקרנו על ענין מציאות הבורא יתברך.

וכן אנו צריכים שנזהר במדותיו אשר ספר בהם עצם כבודו ואשר ספרוהו בהם נביאיו שלא לחשוב אותם כנראה מהמלות ומה שיורה עליהם פירושם הגשמי.

אך צריך שנדע ידיעה ברורה כי הם על דרך העברות ומליצות בפי כח הכרתנו ויכולת תבונתנו ושכלנו מפני דוחק צרכנו לדעתו ולרוממו. והוא יתברך גדול ומרומם מכל זה עד אין תכלית וכמו שאמר הכתוב (נחמיה ט) ומרומם על כל ברכה ותהלה.

ואמר אחד מן הפילוסופים מי שקצר שכלו להבין ענין הפשיטות החזיק בשמות אשר דברו בהם הספרים הנתונים מאת הבורא ולא ידע כי המליצה בספרי התורות לא תהיה אלא כפי בינת מי שניתנו להם לא כפי מה שמליצין בו על המדבר אליהם אך הם כמו השריקה לבהמה בעת שתות המים שמביאתה לשתות יותר ממה שהיה הדבור עושה הצח והנבון.

וכאשר תעמוד על המעלה הזאת מן היחוד בשכלך ותבונתך, יחד נפשך לבורא יתעלה והשתדל להשיג מציאותו מצד חכמתו וגבורתו וחנותו ורחמנותו ורוב

הטעם בלבד והחום והקור והרבה מעניני האיכות בחוש המשוש.

ולכל חוש מהם כח להשיג מוחשו עד גבול ידוע מגיע אצלו ואחר יעמוד בתכלית הגבול ההוא כראות שהוא משיג הדבר הנראה מקרוב וכל אשר ירחק ממנו תחלש השגתו אותו עד שתעמוד ולא ישיגהו וכן חוש השמע וכן שאר החושים ואי אפשר להשיג מוחש מבלעדי חושו המוכן לו.

ומי שיטרח להשיגהו בזולתו לא יגיע אל חפצו כמו מי שיטרח להשיג הנגון בחוש ראותו והמראים בחוש שמעו והטעמים בחוש משושו. לא יוכל למצאם ולהשיגם ואם הם נמצאים. מפני שמבקשם בבלעדי האברים אשר בהם יושגו.

וכן נאמר בחושים הנפשיים אשר זכרנו שיש לכל חוש מהם כח מיוחד להשיג מוחש מיוחד לא יושג בזולתו והגבול אשר יגיע החוש אליו יעמוד אצלו כמו שזכרנו בחושים הגשמיים.

וכן נאמר בשכל שהוא משיג הדברים המושכלים בעצמו ובדרך הראיות מה שהוא קרוב אליו ישיגהו באמתת עצמו ומה שהוא רחוק ונעלם ממנו ישיגהו בדרך הראיות המורות עליו.

וכיון שהבורא ית' נעלם מכל נעלם ורחוק מכל רחוק מצד עצם כבודו אצלנו לא תשיג השכל זולתי ענין מציאותו בלבד.

ואם ישתדל להשיג אמתת עצם כבודו או לדמותו תהיה מציאותו נעדרת ממנו אחר המצאו מפני שהשתדל בדבר שאיננו ביכלתו. כמו שספרנו מהעדר המוחש הגשמי כשמבקשים אותו בבלתי החוש המוכן לו.

ועל כן אנחנו צריכין לבקש מציאות הבורא יתברך מצד סימני מעשיו בברואים ויהיו לנו לראיות עליו וכשתתקיים לנו מציאותו מן הדרך הזה אנחנו צריכין שנעמוד ולא נבקש במחשבותינו לדמותו ולא ברעיונינו לשום לו תבנית ולהמשילו ולהשיג הוית עצם כבודו. ואם נעשה כן ואנו חושבים להקריבו אל בינתנו אז תעדר ממנו מציאותו. כי כל המתדמה במחשבותינו הוא ענין זולתו ואמר הכתוב (משלי כה) דבש מצאת אכול דיך פן תשבענו והקאותו:

וראיתי לקרב לך הענין הזה בשני דמיונים קרובים,

האחד מהם יורך כי כל חוש משיג מוחשו ואחר יעמוד ויתחיל חוש אחר סמוך לו ואחר יעמוד גם הוא וכן שאר החושים. וכשיעמדו יתחיל השכל להשיג מה שיש בכחו להשיג. וכל זה בעניין אחד בעצמו,

והוא שתתחשוב באבן מושלכת מרחוק עשתה צליל והכתה אדם אחד השיג בחוש ראותו מראה האבן ודמותה והשיג בחוש שמעו צליל אבן והשיג בחוש משושו

ונאמר על קצת מן החכמים שהיה אומר בתפלתו אלהי אנה אמצאך אך אנה לא אמצאך נסתרת ולא תראה והכל ממך מלא. דומה למה שאמר יתברך (ירמיה כג) את השמים ואת הארץ אני מלא נאם ה'.

ותכלית דעתך אותו שתודה ותאמין שאתה בתכלית הסכלות באמתת עצם כבודו.

וכשתדמה לו צורה במחשבתך או המשל ברעיונך השתדל לחקור על ענינו,

אז תתברר לך מציאותו,

ותדחה ממחשבתך דמותו עד שלא תמצאהו אלא בדרך הראיות בלבד.

והדמיון בזה על דרך הקירוב מצאנו אמתת הנפש מבלי שנשיג ממנה צורה ולא דמות ולא מראה ולא ריח אע"פ שפעולותיה נראות ומעשיה ניכרים בנו.

וכן השכל שפעולותיו וסימניו נכרים ונראים לא נשיג ממנו דמות ולא צורה ולא נמשילהו ברעיוננו,

כל שכן יוצר הכל אשר אין כמוהו ית'. ואמר הפילוסוף אם הדברים יגעים בענין הנפש ק"ו בענין הבורא יתעלה.

וכיון שהגענו עד הנה מדברינו אין צורך לבאר העניין הזה יותר,

מפני שאנו חייבין לרהות ולירא ולהזהר ממנו כמו שאמר קצת החכמים במופלא ממך אל תדרוש ובמכוסה ממך אל תחקור במה שהורשת התבונן ואין לך עסק בנסתרות,

ואמרו רז"ל כל מי שלא חס על כבוד קונו ראוי לו כאלו לא בא לעולם ואמרו בהיסופר לו כי אדבר אם אמר איש כי יבולע (איוב לו) אם בא אדם לספר גבורתו של מקום מתבלע מן העולם ואמר הכתוב (ש"א ו) ויך באנשי בית שמש כי ראו בארון ה' ואמר (משלי כה) כבוד אלהים הסתר דבר רוצה לומר להסתיר סודו מבני אדם שאינם חכמים ואמר (תהלים כה) סוד ה' ליראיו:

וממה שצריך שתדע ויתבאר אצלך מענין החושים הגשמיים אשר זכרנו והחושים הנפשיים אשר הם הזכרון והמחשבה והרעיון והזמה וההכרה שכולם מגיעים עד ענין אחד והוא השכל הנותן להם כח להשגת הענינים,

ולכל חוש מהם ענין מיוחד להשיג מוחשו לא יושג בזולתו. כמראים והצורות אשר לא נשיגם כי אם בחוש הראות בלבד וכהקולות והנגונים אשר לא נשיגם כי אם בחוש השמע בלבד וכן הריח ומיני המורחים בחוש האף וכן מיני המטעמים בחוש

(דברים לב) הצור תמים פעלו כי כל דרכיו משפט ואמר עוד (שם י) הוא אלהי
האלהים ואדוני האדונים האל הגדול הגבור והנורא וגו' ואמר (שם) עושה משפט
יתום ואלמנה וגר ואמר הוא יתעלה בספור מדותיו (שמות לד) ה' ה' אל רחום וחנון
ארך אפים ורב חסד ואמת נוצר חסד לאלפים וגו'.

וכל אלה המדות הראיה עליהם מסימני מעשיו בבריאותיו והחכמה והיכולת
הנראות במעשיו אם נחקור על הענין הזה בשכלנו והכרתנו נלאה מהשיג הקטן
שבקטנים מחלקי מדותיו ושבחיו כמו שאמר דהמע"ה (תהלים מ) רבות עשית אתה
ה' אלהי נפלאותיך ומחשבותיך אלינו וגו'. ואמר (שם קו) מי ימלל גבורות ה' ישמיע
כל תהלתו ואמר (נחמיה ט) ויברכו שם כבודך ומרומם על כל ברכה ותהלה וכבר
אמרו ז"ל,

ההוא שלוחא דצבורא דנחית קמיה דרבי חנינא אמר האל הגדול הגבור והנורא
העזוז החזק והאמיץ אמר ליה סיימתינהו לכלהו שבחי דמרך ומה האל הגדול
והנורא אי לאו דמשה אמרינהו ואתו אנשי כנסת הגדולה ותקנינהו בתפלה
לא הוה אמרינן להו ואת שבחתיה כולי האי משל למלך שהיה לו אלף אלפים
דינרי זהב והיו מקלסים אותו בשל כסף והלא גנאי הוא לו,

ואמר (תהלים סה) לך דומיה תהלה אלהים בציון ואמרו קדמונינו ז"ל סמא דכולא
משתוקא משל למרגניתא דלית בה טימי כל כמה דאת משבח לה את מגנה לה,

על כן אתה צריך להטריח נפשך עד שתדע את בוראך מצד יתעלה מצד סימני מעשיו
ולא מצד עצם כבודו כי הוא קרוב מכל קרוב מצד פעולותיו ורחוק מכל רחוק מצד
דמות עצם כבודו והמשלו כי לא נוכל למצאו במחשבתנו מן הצד הזה אשר
הקדמנו וכשתגיע להוציאו ממחשבותיך והרגשותיך מפני שאינו נמצא ומצאת
אותו מצד סימני פעולותיו כאילו אינו נפרד ממך מזה היא תכלית ידיעתו אשר
הזהיר הנביא עליה באמרו (דברים ד) וידעת היום והשבות אל לבבך כי ה' הוא
האלהים וגו',

ואמר אחד מן החכמים היודע את הבורא דעת יתירה הוא נבהל בעניניו יותר,

ואמר אחד החכם שבבני אדם בדעת הבורא הוא יותר סכל באמתת עצם כבודו
ומי שאינו יודע אותו הוא סבור שיודע עצם כבודו:

ונשאל קצת החכמים על הבורא מהו ואמר אלוה אחד א"ל השואל ואיך הוא א"ל
מלך גדול א"ל ואנה הוא א"ל בצפיה,

א"ל השואל לא שאלתיך על זה,

א"ל שאלתני במלות האלה שמורות על המדות הראויות לנברא ולא על בורא. אך
המדות שצריך להבין מבוראנו יתעלה מה שאמרתי לך מפני שא"א לנו זולת זה.

ואפשר שנודע אליהם בעבור התיחדם בעבודתו בדורם מפני שהיו אנשי דורם עובדים לאלהים אחרים,

וכן נאמר בהקראו (שמות ג) אלהי העברים (בראשית לג) אלהי ישראל כמ״ש הכתוב (ירמיה י) לא כאלה חלק יעקב כי יוצר הכל הוא,

ואמר דוד (תהלים טז) ה׳ מנת חלקי וכוסי אתה תומיך גורלי ואלו היינו יכולים להשיג אמתת ענינו לא היה נודע אלינו בזולתה,

וכיון שנמנעה משכלנו השגת אמתת ענינו ספר עצם כבודו שהוא אלהי מבחר יצוריו מדברים ושאינם מדברים. ועל כן אמר למשה רבינו ע״ה בעת ששאלו (שמות ג) ואמרו לי מה שמו מה אומר אליהם ויאמר כה תאמר לבני ישראל אהיה שלחני אליכם וכיון שידע שהשם הזה לא יבין העם ממנו אמתת ענינו הוסיף באור ואמר כה תאמר אל בני ישראל ה׳ אלהי אבותיכם אלהי אברהם אלהי יצחק ואלהי יעקב שלחני אליכם זה שמי לעלם וזה זכרי לדר דר.

והיה רצונו בזה אם לא יבין העם המלות האלו וענינם בדרך שכלם אמור להם שאני הוא הידוע אצלם מצד הקבלה שקבלו מאבותם מפני שלא שם הבורא דרך לדעתו זולתי אלה השני דרכים. האחד מה שהשכל מראה מדרך אותות פעולותיו הנראות בבריאותיו. והשני מצד הקבלה מן האבות כמו שאמר הכתוב (איוב טו) אשר חכמים יגידו ולא כחדו מאבותם:

ומפני שהיתה השגתנו לכל נמצא על אחד משלשה צדדים.

האחד מהם הרגשותינו הגשמיים כראות וכשמע וכטעם וכריח וכמשוש.

והשני בדרך שכלנו והוא שער הראיה על הדבר הנמצא מסימניו ומעשיו עד שתתקיים לנו אמתת מציאותו וענינו ממנו כקיום השגתנו בהרגשותינו,

והוא הנקרא בספר דעת ומוסר השכל.

והשלישי ההגדה האמתית והקבלה הנאמנת.

ומפני שנמנעת השגת הבורא מצד הרגשותינו לא יכלנו להשיגו אלא מצד ההגדה האמתית ומצד הראיה עליו מאותות מעשיו בלבד.

וכיון שעמדו לנו הראיות מצד אותות פעולותיו בברואים ורבו מספריהם רבו ספורי מדותיו יתעלה בעבורם,

וספרוהו הנביאים והחסידים בספורים שאין דומים זה לזה. אמר משה רבינו ע״ה

וכן נאמר בבאור החכמה הצפונה אשר כווננו לבארה בספר הזה כי התורה קצרה בבאור ענינה מפני שסמכה בו על השכל ורמזה ממנה ברמזים להעיר עליהם כבר זכרנום בתחלת הספר הזה להתעורר אליה כל מי שיוכל לחקור עליה ולדרוש אותה כדי שיגיע אליה ויבינה כמ"ש (משלי כח) ומבקשי ה' יבינו כל.

וכבר הזהירנו הנביא שנשמר מחשוב שיש לה' צורה או דמיון כמ"ש (דברים ד) ונשמרתם מאד לנפשותיכם כי לא ראיתם כל תמונה ואמר (שם) ותמונה אינכם רואים זולתי קול ר"ל הזהרו במחשבותיכם ורעיוניכם שלא תמשילו לבורא יתעלה תבנית ולא תדמוהו בדמות ולא דמיון מפני שלא נפלו עיניכם על דמות ולא על צורה בעת שדבר עמכם,

ואמר (ישעיה מ) ואל מי תדמיון אל ומה דמות תערכו לו ואמר (שם) ואל מי תדמיוני ואשוה יאמר קדוש,

ונאמר (תהלים פט) כי מי בשחק יערוך לה' ידמה לה' בבני אלים ואמר (שם פו) אין כמוך באלהים ה' ואין כמעשיך והרבה כזה.

ומפני שנמנע לדמותו בשכל ולהמשילו ברעיון מצאנו בספר הזה שהוא מיחס רוב שבחיו ותהלותיו אל שם הבורא כמ"ש (נחמיה ט) ויברכו שם כבודך (דברים כח) ליראה את השם הנכבד והנורא (תהלים צט) יודו שמך גדול ונורא ואמר (מלאכי ב) ומפני שמי נחת הוא (שם ג) וזרחה לכם יראי שמי שמש צדקה וגו' (תהלים סח) שירו לאלהים זמרו שמו סולו לרוכב בערבות ביה שמו,

וכל זה לגדל ולרומם עצם כבודו ית' מפני שאין מתברר במחשבתנו מענינו אחר מציאותו זולתי שמו הגדול בלבד,

אבל עצם כבודו ואמתת ענינו אין לו דמות ותמונה במחשבתנו ועל כן שנה במקומות רבים בספר התורה שמו וכן בספרי הנביאים,

כי לא נבין ממנו בלתי שמו ומציאותו וכבר צרפו שם כבודו אל השמים ואל הארץ ואל הרוחות כמו שאמר אברהם (בראשית כד) ואשביעך בה' אלהי השמים ואלהי הארץ ואמר יונה (בסימן א) את ה' אלהי השמים אני ירא ואמר משה רבינו ע"ה (במדבר כז) יפקוד ה' אלהי הרוחות לכל בשר ואמר הכתוב (ירמיה לב) אני ה' אלהי כל בשר.

והעילה בזה כי הוא נודע אלינו מן הצד אשר ממנו ידענוהו והשכלנו ענינו ומציאותו נודע אלינו הרבה מצד אבותינו כמ"ש (שמות ג) ה' אלהי אבותיכם אלהי אברהם אלהי יצחק ואלהי יעקב שלחני אליכם זה שמי לעלם. והעילה בזה שנודע אלינו מן הצד שעמדנו עליו והוא קבלת אבותינו אשר ירשנו מהם דרכיו כמ"ש (בראשית יח) כי ידעתיו למען אשר יצוה את בניו ואת ביתו אחריו ושמרו דרך ה' לעשות צדקה ומשפט,

נצטרך עמו לפרשם ולבארם בספר הזה. ואשר נסכים עליו כלנו כי הדחק הביאנו
להגשים הבורא ית׳ ולספר אותו במדות הברואים כדי לשער ענין שיקיים מציאות
הבורא יתב׳ בנפשות והוציאו אותו ספרי הנביאים לב״א במלות גשמיות שהם
קרובות לשכלם ולהבנתם,

ואלו היו מספרים אותו בענין שראוי לו מן המלות הרוחניות והענינים הרוחניים לא
היינו מבינים לא המלות ולא הענין ולא היה אפשר שנעבוד דבר שלא נדע כי לא
יתכן עבודת דבר שאינו נודע ע״כ היה צריך שתהיינה המלות והענינים כפי כח
בינת השומע כדי שיפול הענין על לבו ע״ד הגשמות המובן מן המלות הגשמיות
בתחלה ואח״כ נתחכם לו ונדקדק להבינו ולהודיעו שכל זה ע״ד הקרבה ומליצת
הספר ושהענין האמתי הוא יותר דק ומעולה ומרומם ורחוק מאשר נוכל להבין
אותו על תכונת דקות ענינו והמשכיל הנלבב ישתדל להפשיט קליפות המלות
וגשמותם מעל הענין ויעלהו במחשבתו ממדרגה אל מדרגה עד שיגיע מאמתת
הענין הנדרש אל מה שיש בכח יכלתו והשגתו,

והכסיל הפתי יחשוב הבורא ית׳ על דרך הנראה ממליצת הספר וכשהוא מקבל
על עצמו עבודת אלהיו והוא משתדל לעשותו לכבודו יש לו טענה גדולה מצד
פתיותו ומעוט הבנתו מפני שאין האדם נתבע אלא כפי יכלתו והשגתו בשכלו
והבנתו וכח וממונו אלא שהכסיל כשאפשר לו ללמוד החכמה ומתעלם ממנה הוא
נתבע עליה ונענש על אשר קצר ועמד מללמוד,

ואלו היה נוהג הספר כשמתרגם הענין הזה המנהג הראוי באמתו אשר לא יוכל
להבינו כי אם המשכיל הנלבב לבד היו נשארים רוב המדברים בלי דת ובלי תורה
מפני קוצר שכלם וחלישות הכרתם בענינים הרוחניים. כי הדבר שיובן ממנו ענין
גשמי לא יזיק המשכיל מפני שהוא מכיר בו ומועיל הכסיל כדי להתישב בלבו
ובדעתו כי יש לו בורא שהוא חייב לו בעבודתו:

וזה דומה לאדם שבא אל אחד מאוהביו מן העשירים והיה חייב בארוחתו והיו לו
בהמות שחייב לתת לחם מספוא ושלח אליו הרבה מן השעורים לבהמותיו ושלח
מן המאכל הראוי לו מעט כפי הצורך והמספיק למזונו בלבד,

וכן הרחיבה לשון הקודש וכל ספרי הנביאים ודברי החסידים במדות הבורא ית׳
במליצות הגשמיות אשר זכרנו כפי הבנת ההמון ובלשון שמדברים בו בני אדם
איש אל רעהו ועל כן אמרו רז״ל בדומה לענין הזה דברה תורה כלשון בני אדם.
ורמזו הספרים במעט מן הענינים הרוחניים אשר יבינום אנשי השכל והלבבות,

להיות הכל שוים בדעת מציאות הבורא יתעלה ואם תתחלק אמתת עצם כבודו
בדעתם,

וכן נאמר בכל ענין רק שיש בספר תורת האלהים כמו גמול העולם הבא וענשו.

כיותר ממלה אחת.

והרבוי הנמצא במדות הבורא יתעלה איננו מצד עצם כבודו רק מצד קוצר כח מליצת המספר מהשיג ענינו במלה אחת שתורה עליו. וצריך שתבין מענין הבורא שאין כמוהו דבר וכל אשר תספר אותו בו מן המדות צריך שתבין מהם ריחוק שכנגדם ממנו. כאשר אמר אריסטו״ו השוללות במדות הבורא ית׳ אמתיות מן המחייבות. מפני שכל מה שמחייבין לעצם כבודו מן המדות איננו נמלט ממדות העצם או ממדות המקרה ובורא העצם והמקרה לא תשיגהו מדה ממדותם בעצם כבודו וכל המרוחקות ממנו מן המדות הן אמיתות בלי ספק והנה נאותות לו כי הוא נעלה מכל מדה ותאר ומרומם מכל דמות ודמיון וע״כ אתה צריך שתבין מן המדות האלה השלש אשר זכרנו הרחקת שכנגדם מעל הבורא יתברך:

אך המדות האלהיות ההפעליות הם המדות אשר יסופר בהן הבורא יתברך מצד פעולותיו ואפשר שישתתף בספורם עם קצת ברואיו והותרנו לספר אותו בהם מפני הדחק המצריך אותנו להודיענו ולעמוד על מציאותו כדי שנקבל עבודתו,

וכבר מצאנו שמשתמשין במין הזה ממדות הבורא בספר התורה ובספרי הנביאים הרבה מאד ובתשבחות הנביאים החסידים והם על שני דרכים.

הדרך האחד מדות שהן מורות על דמות וצורה גשמית כמו שאמר הכתוב (בראשית א) ויברא אלהים את האדם בצלמו בצלם אלהים ברא אותו (שם ט) כי בצלם אלהים עשה את האדם (במדבר ט) על פי ה׳ (ישעיה מה) אני ידי נטו שמים (במדבר יא) באזני ה׳ (שמות כד) ותחת רגליו (ישעיה נא) זרוע ה׳ (תהלים כד) אשר לא נשא לשוא נפשי (בראשית ו) בעיני ה׳ (שם ח) ויאמר ה׳ אל לבו והדומה לזה מן האברים הגופיים.

והשני מדות שהן מורות על תנועות ומעשים גשמיים כמו שנאמר (שם) וירח ה׳ (שם ו) וירא (שם) וינחם (שם) ויתעצב אל לבו (שם יא) וירד ה׳ (שם ח) ויזכור אלהים (במדבר יא) וישמע ה׳ (תהלים עח) ויקץ כישן ה׳ ורבים כאלה ממעשי המדברים.

אלא שקדמונינו ז״ל בפרשם כתבי הקדש תרגמו לנו המין הזה מן המדות ודקדקו בו כפי יכלתם להבינם דרך כבוד וייחסו הכל אל כבוד הבורא יתברך כאשר תרגמו (בראשית כח) והנה ה׳ נצב עליו והא יקרא דה׳ מעתד עלוהי (שם ו) וירא ה׳ וגלי קדם ה׳ (שם יא) וירד ה׳ ואתגלי יקרא דה׳ (שם לה) ויעל מעליו אלהים ואסתלק מעלוהי יקרא דה׳,

הוציאו את הכל דרך כבוד והרחיקו אותם מהבורא יתברך כדי שלא ישיגהו שום הגשמה ולא שום מקרה.

וכבר האריך בבאור הענין הזה הגאון הגדול רבינו סעדיה ז״ל בספר האמונות ובפירוש ספר בראשית ובפירוש ספר וארא ובספר יצירה מה שיש בו די ושלא

העולם יתעלה לא מתרבה ולא נעדר ולא מחודש,

וכן צריך שתדע כי כל אחת מאלות המדות השלש אשר זכרנו מחייבת שאריתם כאשר נתבונן בעניניהם.

ובאור זה כי האחד האמת כשהוא דבק וקיים בשום דבר צריך על כל פנים שיהיה נמצא קדמון מפני שהתברר כי הנעדר לא יסופר בא׳ ולא ברוב וכשיאות לשום דבר ענין האחד האמת ויתקיים לו דין הוא שיאות לו שם המציאות ועינה וכן ענין הקדמות דבק לו מפני שאחד האמת לא יתהווה ולא יפסד ולא ישתנה ולא יתחלף א״כ הוא קדמון כיון שאין לו תחלה. ומי שהתקיים לו ענין האחדות האמתית כבר התקיים (ס״א התברר) לו ענין המציאות והקדמות.

וכן נאמר כי מדת המציאות התמידית כשהיא נאותה לדבר תאות לו עמה מדת הא׳ האמת ומדת הקדמות.

אך מה שראוי לו מטרת האחד מפני שהנמצא תדיר לא יתכן שיהיה נמצא אחד אפס ולא ישתנה מענין המציאה אל אפס מציאה ולא מאפס מציאה אל מציאה ומה שהוא במדה הזאת איננו רב מפני שהרב לא ימצא מציאה תדירה מפני הקדמת האחד לו וכל הנמצא תדיר איננו רב א״כ הוא אחד.

וכן ראויה לו עוד מדת הקדמות כי הנמצא תדיר אין לו תחלה ולא תכלה א״כ ענין הקדמות דבק לו עכ״פ.

וכן נאמר כי מדת הקדמות מחייבת למי שהיא ראויה לו מדת האחד האמת ומדת המציאות התדירה,

ומה שראוי לו ממדת האחד האמת מפני שהנמצא תדיר הוא שאין לו תחלה ומה שאין לו תחלה איננו מתרבה שכל מתרבה יש לו תחלה והוא האחד א״כ אין המתרבה קדמון והקדמון לא יתכן שיהיה אלא אחד והתחייבה מדת הא׳ בחיוב מדת הקדמות,

וכן צריך שתתחייב מדת המציאות בהתחייב מדת הקדמות כי האפס לא יסופר לא בקדמון ולא בחדש.

וכבר התבאר כי המדות האלה השלש ענינם אחד והנראה מהן אחד ושאינן מחייבות שנוי לעצם כבוד הבורא יתעלה ולא הכנסת המקרים עליו ולא הרבוי על ענינו מפני שהענין אשר נבין מהם הוא שהבורא יתעלה איננו נעדר ולא חדש ולא מתרבה ואילו היינו יכולין להליץ על ענינו במלה א׳ הכוללת אלו המדות בבת אחת. כמו שכולל אותם השכל כדי שיעלו אלו השלשה ענינים בדעתנו בה כאשר הם עולים בשלש אשר זכרנו היינו מליצים בה עליו. וכיון שלא מצאנו במה שאנו מדברים בו מן הלשונות מלה שתורה על אמתת ענין הבורא ית׳ הוצאנו הענין

~~ פרק י ~~

אך באור המדות האלהיות המושכלות והכתובות המסופר בהן הבורא יתברך הכוונות בהם רבות מאד בפי רוב הברואים והטובות הכוללות אותן,

והן מתחלקות לשני חלקים עצמיות ופעליות.

וטעם אמרנו עצמיות שהן מדות קיימות לאל יתעלה קודם הברואים ואחריהם תאותנה לו לעצם כבודו,

והן שלש מדות והן,

שהוא נמצא,

ושהוא אחד,

ושהוא קדמון אין לו ראשית.

והטעם שאנו מספרים אותו באלה המדות להורות על ענינו ואמתת מציאותו ולהעיר על כבודו ולהבין המדברים כי יש להם בורא שחייבין בעבודתו,

והוצרכנו לספר אותו בנמצא מפני שהראיות הורו על מציאותו בעדות סימני מעשיו בעולם כמו שנאמר (ישעיה מ) שאו מרום עיניכם וראו מי ברא אלה המוציא במספר צבאם לכלם בשם יקרא מרוב אונים ואמיץ' כח איש לא נעדר,

ע"כ נתחייבנו לספר אותו בנמצא מפני שהתקיים בשכלנו כי הנעדר לא יהיה ממנו פעל ולא שום מעשה. וכיון שהתבררו מעשיו ובריאותיו התברר בדעתנו מציאותו,

אך מה שאנו מספרים אותו בו מן הקדמות מפני שהראיות הורו כי לעולם הזה ראשון אין לפניו לפניו ותחלה שאין תחלה לפניה והתברר כי ההתחלות א"א שתהיינה מאין תכלית מנין בתחלתן והדין נותן על כל פנים שהבורא יתעלה ראשון אין לפניו לפניו וזהו ענין הקדמות כמו שאמר (תהלים צ) ומעולם עד עולם אתה אל ונאמר (ישעיה מג) לפני לא נוצר אל ואחרי לא יהיה.

אך מה שנספר עליו שהוא אחד כבר באר בארנו זה באר היטב בראיות ידועות והתקיים בעדיות ברורות כי הענין האחדות האמתי דבק אל עצם כבודו וענין האחד ריחוק הרבוי מעצם מעצמו בכבודו והמנע השנוי והחלוף והמקרה וההויה וההפסד והחבור והפרידה והדמיון והשתוף מאמתת עצם כבודו ושאר גדרי הרב:

וצריך שתבין מן המדות האלה שהן לא תחייבנה לעצם כבוד הבורא שגוי וחלוף אך ענינם להרחיק זולתם ממנו יתעלה והעולה על דעתנו ושכלנו מענינם כי בורא

וכאשר חקרנו על ענין האחדות האמתית בברואים לא מצאנוה לאחד מהם קיימת אמתית ואם יאמר [על כל אחד מן הסוגים והמינים והאישים והעצמים והמקרים והגרמים העליונים והגופים הרוחניים וכל מנין ומנוי וכל אשר לו תכלה וגבול] אחד ומיחסים אליו ענין האחדות לא יאמר לו אחד אלא על דרך העברה מפני שהוא כולל דברים שנקראו אחד מדרך הדמותם והתחברותם בענין אחד,

והוא רב מעצמו מפני שמקבל הרבוי והשנוי והחלוק והמחלוקת והחבור והפרידה והתוספת והחסרון והתנועה והמנוחה והדמיון והצורה ושאר המקרים המיוחדים והכוללים לכל אחד מהברואים,

והאחדות האמתית איננה נמצאת ולא נאמרת באמת על דבר מן היצירות. ומפני שהיה האחד נמצא בברואים בדרך המקרה והורה האות והמופת כי הבורא אחד. ידענו דעת ברורה כי האחדות אשר אמרנו על כל אחד מהברואים על דרך העברה נאצלת מענין האחד האמת האמת והאחדות האמתית היא הנאמרת על בורא הכל יתעלה והוא האחד האמת ואין אחד אמת זולתו כמו שהקדמנו.

וכל חקי האחד האמת אשר זכרנו לא יאותו כי אם לו לבדו וכן כל עניני הרבוי והמקרים והשנוים והתנועות והדמיונים וכל מה שלא יאות לאחד האמת רחוקים ממנו יתברך כמ"ש דוד ע"ה (תהלים מ) רבות עשית אתה ה' אלהי נפלאותיך ומחשבותיך אלינו אין ערוך אליך וגו' ואמר הכתוב (ישעיה מ) ואל מי תדמיון אל ומה דמות תערכו לו ונאמר (תהלים פו) אין כמוך באלהים ה' ואין כמעשיך ונאמר (ירמיה י) מאין כמוך ה' גדול אתה וגדול שמך בגבורה וגו'.

וכבר התבאר והתברר כי בורא העולם יתברך אחד אמת ושאין אחד אמת זולתו כי כל מה שיפול עליו שם אחד זולת הבורא אם הוא אחד מצד אחד הוא רב מצד אחר כאשר זכרנו אך הבורא א' מכל פנים כמו שבארנו ובמה שהבאנו בענין הזה די למבין:

~~ פרק ט ~~

אך הראיה שהבורא יתברך אחד אמת אין אחד אמת זולתו נאמר

כי מפני שכל מחובר לא תגמר הויתו אלא בהשתתף חלקיו אשר חובר מהם והוא התאחד קצתם עם קצתם ועיקר השיתוף האחדות.

וכן לא יתכן מציאות המחובר אלא בהתחלק חלקיו אשר מהם חובר כי החבור לא יהיה כי אם מדברים שהם יותר מאחד ועיקר המחלוקת הרב וכיון שהיה סימן החבור וההרכבה והסדור נמצא בעוה"ז

בכלליו בפרטיו וחלקיו ושרשיו וענפיו צריך שימצא בכלם ענין השתוף והמחלוקת ועיקרם האחדות והרב.

ומפני שהאחדות קודמת לרב נטבע כקדימת האחד לשאר המנין מן הדין שתהיה עילת כל מתרבה בלתי מתרבה בראש ההתחלות מפני הקדמת ענין האחדות לכל מתרבה,

וכיון שהיו העילות מגיעות בתחלתן ונמנע שיפעל הפועל בעצמו לא היה אפשר שתהיה עילת האחדות והרב כמותן רב ואחדות,

וכיון שאין עילת ההויות הרב בלבד ולא רב ואחדות. מן הדין שיהיה עילת ההויה אחד אמת.

וכבר הקדמנו בדברינו כי העילות כל אשר תעלינה למעלה תתמעטנה בתחלתן עד אשר תהיינה מגיעות אל שרש המנין והוא אחד האמת והוא הבורא יתברך.

ומן הידוע עוד כי כל מה שימצא בשום דבר מקרה אי אפשר שלא ימצא בדבר אחר עצמי אמתי ואין לו העתקה ממנו כי אם בהפסדו כחום במים החמים שהוא מקרה במים והוא באש עצמי קיים,

ומן הידוע עוד כי כל מה שימצא בשום דבר מקרה אין הדבר ההוא אשר יקרה בו המקרה מקבל אותו המקרה אלא מן הדבר אשר הוא בו עצמי כמו שאנחנו רואים בחום המים שהוא מקרה בהם נאצל עליהם מן האש שחומה עצמי בה. וכאשר אנחנו רואים מלחות הדברים הלחים במקרה שנאצל עליהם מן המים שהלחות בהם עצמית וכן שאר כל ההויות כאשר נסתכל בענייניהם.

ועל ההקשה הזאת ננהיג דברינו בענין האחדות כי כיון שהיתה בכל אחד מהברואים מקרית כאשר הקדמנו מן הדין הוא שתהיה בעילת הברואים עצמית קיימת אמתות וממנה קבלו כל ההויות ענין האחדות בדרך המקרה כאשר ארנו

והענין השני אשר הוא אחר אמתי נמצא בפעל. הוא ענין אשר לא יתרבה ולא ישתנה ולא יתחלף ולא יסופר במדה ממדות הגשמיים ולא תשיגהו לא הויה ולא הפסד ולא תכלה. ולא יעתק ולא ינוע ולא ידמה אל דבר ולא ידמה אליו דבר ולא ישתתף עם דבר. כי הוא עכ"פ אחד אמת והוא שרש לכל מתרבה כאשר עבר מדברינו. כי האחדות עילת הרבוי,

ואין לאחד האמתי תחלה ולא תכלית. כי כל מה שיש לו תחלה ותכלה מן הדין שתכנס ההויה וההפסד עליו וכל מה שתכנס ההויה וההפסד עליו משתנה והשני כנגד האחדות א"כ יהיה יותר מאחד כי הוא קודם ההתחלה לזולתו אחריה וזה מחייב לו הרבוי,

וכן הדמות במתדמה מקרה וכל אשר ישיגנו מקרה מתרבה והאחד האמת לא ישיגהו שום מקרה בעצם כבודו בשום פנים.

ואם יאמר אומר שהאחדות באחד האמת מקרה,

נאמר כי ענין האחדות באחד האמת הוא הרחקת הרבוי והרב ממנו וכאשר נספר האחד לא נספרהו כי אם בענין אפיסת הרבוי והרב. והאחד האמת לא יסופר במדה שמחייבת לעצם כבודו רבוי ולא שנוי ולא חלוף בשום פנים. ובזה נשלמו כל דברינו באחד העובר והאחד האמת ואתה דע לך:

~~ פרק ח ~~

אך באור אופני האחד האמתי והאחד העובר,

הוא שהאחד שם נגזר מן האחדות והוא נאמר על שני ענינים. האחד מהם מקרי והוא העובר והשני עצמי קיים והוא האמתי,

והאחד המקרי גם כן הוא על שני ענינים. האחד מהם נראה בו הרבוי והכלל והקבוץ כסוג האחד אשר הוא כולל מינים רבים וכמין האחד הכולל אישים רבים וכאיש הא׳ המחובר מחלקים רבים וכצבא האחד הכולל אנשים רבים,

וכאמרנו כור אחד והין א׳ ורובע א׳ וליטרא אחת וכל א׳ מהם כולל דברים רבים יאמר על כ״א מהם א׳. וכל א׳ ממה שהזכרנו נקרא אחד על דרך העברה והוא מפני שהדברים ההם אשר יקבץ אותם השם ההוא שוים בענין א׳ ונקרא רב מפני שכולל דברים רבים וכאשר יתפרדו הדברים ההם ויתבודדו יאמר על כל אחד מהם אחד והאחד בכמו העניני האלה אשר זכרנו מקרה והוא אחד מצד ורב מצד.

והענין השני מאחד המקרי הוא האחד הנאמר על האיש הא׳ לא מתרבה ולא כולל דברים רבים כנראה ממנו אך הוא רב בעצמו מצד חבורו מחומר וצורה ועצם ומקרה, והוא מקבל ההויה וההפסד והחלוק והחבור והפרידה והשנוי והחלוף והשתוף.

אם כן הרבוי ישיג הדבר הנאמר עליו אחד מכל מה שספרנו מפני שהם כנגד האחדות. כי האחד הנאמר על הדבר אשר ישיגנו בעצמו ענין מעניני הרבוי והשנוי הוא מקרה מבלי ספק והוא אחד על דרך העברה לא ע״ד האמת. שים לבך להבין:

אך האחד האמת יאמר גם כן על שני פנים. האחד מהם במחשבה והשני בפעל.

והמחשבה הוא האחד המניני אשר הוא שרש כל מנין ותחלתו וטעם האחד המניני שהוא אות וסימן לתחלה שאין תחלה לפניה כי כל תחלה אמתית תקרא אחד כמו שנאמר (בראשית א) ויהי ערב ויהי בקר יום אחד במקום יום ראשון הוציאו בלשון אחד מפני שהאחד שם לתחלה שאין לפניה תחלה וכשהוא שונה יקרא שני וכשהוא משלש יקרא שלישי וכן עד עשרה ואחר כן ישוב אל האחד ואחר כן ישוב אל מאה ואל אלף אין תכלית למנין.

וע״כ היה גדר המנין כלל מורכב מן האחרים והטעם שקראתיו מחשבי מפני שהמנין אינו נכנס תחת החושים הגשמיים אבל יושג במחשבה. אך המנוי הוא מורגש בחושים הגשמיים החמשה או במקצתם.

א"כ אין הבורא יותר מאחד ואלו היה אפשר להיות יותר מאחד היה אפשר
שתהיה ביניהם מחלוקת בבריאת הברואים ולא היתה נגמרת מהם יצירת
הברואים. ובמצאנו כל העולם הזה על סדר אחד ותנועה אחת נמצאת בכל חלק
מחלקיו לא נשתנה ועם הדורות נדע שיוצרו ומנהיגו אחד לא ישנה מעשהו ולא
יחליף הנהגתו זולתו כמו שאמר (ישעיה מד) ומי כמוני יקרא ויגידה ויערכה לי וגו'.
ואמר דוד (תהלים קיט) לעולם ה' דברך נצב בשמים לדור ודור אמונתך כוננת ארץ
ותעמוד.

ומה שאנו רואים הנהגת הבורא השלמה בברואים כי ההנהגה לא תהיה שלמה
מתמדת על ענין אחד אלא בהתיחד אחד בעצה ובהנהגה כמלך במדינה והנפש
בגוף.

ואמר אריסטו"ו בספרו בענין היחוד אין טוב ברבות הראשים אך הראש האחד
ואמר שלמה (משלי כח) בפשע ארץ רבים שריה וגר,

ובמה שהבאנו בענין הזה די למבין ומספיק בתשובה על הנחת הרבוי בי
בהעמידנו האחדות לבורא העולם תדחה טענת כל מי שיאמר שהוא יותר מאחד
ואתה דע לך:

העולם קדמון והוא עלת העלות ותחלת התחלות והוא על כל פנים אחד והוא
כמ"ש הכתוב (נחמיה ט) אתה הוא ה' לבדך:

והחמישי מצד ענין הרבוי והאחדות והוא שאקליד"ס גדר האחדות בספרו ואמר כי
האחדות היא אשר בה יאמר לכל דבר אחד ר"ל כי האחדות קודמת לאחד
בטבעה כאשר נאמר כי החום קודם לכל דבר חם ולולא האחדות לא היה נאמר
על דבר מהדברים אחד,

והענין אשר אנחנו צריכין להעלות על דעתנו מן האחדות הוא יחידות גמורה
ובדידות שאין עמה חבור ולא דמיון בשום ענין ולא רבוי ולא מספר בשום פנים
ולא התחבר אל דבר ולא התפרד מדבר,

וענין הרבוי הוא כלל אחדים ולא יתכן שיקדים הרבוי לאחדות אשר ממנה נתרבה.
ואם נמצא בשכלנו או בהרגשותינו שום רבוי נדע נדע ידיעה ברורה כי האחדות
קדמתו כקדימת האחד המניני לשאר המנין. ומי שיחשוב כי הבורא יותר מאחד
יש לו לומר על כל פנים כי האחד קודם לכלם מפני הקדמת האחד למנין ואחדות
לרב אם כן הבורא אחד על כל פנים קדמון אין קדמון זולתו כמו שנאמר (ישעיה מג)
לפני לא נוצר אל ואחרי לא יהיה:

והששי מצד המקרים הדבקים אל כל מתרבה והוא שהרבוי והכלל מקרה נכנס על
העצם והוא הכמות והוא יתברך הבורא העצם והמקרה לא תשיגנו מדה ממדותם
בעצם כבודו וכאשר התברר כי הבורא התעלה מכל דמיון וערך אל דבר
מבריאותיו מן השכל ומן הכתוב כי הבורא הנכנס על עצם המתרבה מקרה לא
יאות שתשיג עצם עצם כבוד הבורא מדה ממדות הרבוי ואם לא יסופר ברוב הוא אחד
על כל פנים מפני שאין בין הרב והאחדות אמצעי א"כ אין הבורא יותר מאחד והוא
אחד עכ"פ כמו שאמרה חנה (שמואל א' ב) אין קדוש כה' כי אין בלתך וגו':

והשביעי כי הבורא אם הוא יותר מאחד יהיה כל אחד מהם יכול לברוא העולם או
לא יכול אלא בעזר חברו.

ואם כל אחד מהם יכול הבורא הא' נוסף מפני שהאחר יכול ואיננו צריך לזולתו
ואם לא ישלם הדבר,

כי אם בהתחברם אין לאחד מהם יכולת שלמה ולא כח גמור מפני שכל א' מהם
נלאה ומקצר וכ"א מהם חלש וכל חלש יש תכלית לכחו ולעצמו. וכל אשר יש לו
תכלית יש לו גבול וכל אשר יש לו גבול מחובר וכל מחובר מחודש וכל מחודש יש
לו מחדש.

אם כן החלש אי אפשר שיהיה קדמון מפני שהקדמון לא תקצר ידו מדבר ולא
יצטרך לעזר זולתו.

אחת יעלה בדעתנו מיד כי כותב אחד כתבו וחברו כי הכתב לא יתכן בפחות מכותב אחד ואלו היה יכול להכתב בפחות מכותב אחר היינו חושבים כן ואע"פ שאפשר שיכתבנו יותר מאחד אין ראוי להעלות על דעתנו כן אלא בראיה שתעיד על ברור הדבר מהתחלף צורת המכתב במקצתו והדומה לזה,

ואם היה הדבר כן אין אנו צריכין לדעתנו פנים בפנים אם אי אפשר לעמוד עליו מן הצד הזה ועמדו לנו הראיות עליו ממעשהו בסדור כתיבתו במקום ראותנו אותו. וידענו ידיעה ברורה כי כותב אחד נמצא יודע מכתב ויכול לכתוב כתבו ולא השתתף בו עמו זולתו מפני סדר חבורו והשואתו מפני שמעשה שני עושים מתחלף ואיננו שוה ומסודר על ערך אחד ומשתנה בתקונו ותכונתו,

וכן נאמר בבורא יתעלה כי מפני שהיו אותות החכמה בבריאותיו מתדמות ושוות הוצרכנו להאמין כי בורא אחד בראם כי אי אפשר למציאות המחודשים מבלעדיו,

ושאיננו דבר נראה בעצם ובמקרה ומפני שאיננו נראה אי אפשר למצאו ולדעתו אלא בדרכי הראיות והבחינות המורות עליו מצד בריאותיו אז תעמוד לנו אמונתנו שהוא נמצא ושהוא אחד קדמון היה ויהיה ראשון ואחרון גבור חכם חי,

ועמדו לנו הראיות עליו במקום עמדנו עליו וראותנו אותו יתעלה מפני שאיננו מענינים הנראים,

על כן הוצרכנו להעלות על דעתנו שבורא אחד בראם כי אי אפשר בלעדיו במציאות המחודשים אך יותר מאחד אפשר בלעדיו ואין צורך אליו על כן מי שיטעון שהוא יותר מאחד לא יתקיימו דבריו אלא בראיה זולת הראיה שהבאנו ואי אפשר להעמידה מפני שהראיות שהן מדרך השכל אינן מכחישות זו את זו,

אך כל הראיות מעידות על אחדותו ומרחיקות ממנו ענין הרבוי והשתתוף והדמיון כאשר אמר ה' ית' (ישעיה מד) היש אלוה מבלעדי ואין צור בל ידעתי ואמר (שם) אני ראשון ואני אחרון ואמר (שם מח) אף ידי יסדה ארץ וימיני טפחה שמים קורא אני אליהם יעמדו יחדו ואמר (שם מה) צדיק ומושיע אין זולתי:

והרביעי שנאמר למי שהוא חושב כי הבורא יותר מאחד לא ימלט שיהיה עצם הכל עצם אחד או שלא יהיה אחד.

ואם יאמר כי העצם אחד אם כן הענין אחד והבורא איננו יותר מאחד.

ואם יאמר כי לכל אחד מהם עצם איננו מעצם אחד נצטרך עכ"פ שיהיה ביניהם הפרש מפני מחלקותם והשתנותם וכל נפרש מוגבל וכל מוגבל יש לו תכלית וכל אשר יש לו תכלית מחובר וכל מחובר מחודש וכל מחודש יש לו מחדש.

ומי שחושב כי הבורא יותר מאחד מצריך שיהיה מחודש וכבר הקדמנו כי בורא

ועוד כי אנחנו מוצאים אותו כי הוא צריך בקיומו ותקונו קצתו אל קצתו ואין חלק ממנו נגמר אלא בחלק אחר כצורך קשקשי השריון וחלקי המטה ואברי גוף האדם ושאר המחוברים קצתם אל קצתם בתקונם והשלמתם.

הלא תראה צורך הירח והכוכבים אל אור השמש וצורך הארץ אל השמים ואל המים וצורך בעלי חיים קצתם אל קצתם כי מקצת מיניהם אוכל מקצתם כדורס מן העופות והדגים וחיות השדה וצורך האדם אל הכל ותקנת הכל באדם וצורך הארצות והפלכים והחכמות והמלאכות קצתם אל קצתם,

והחכמה נראית בקטני היצירות וגדוליהם. כי כח החכמה הנראית ביצירת הפיל לפי גודל גופו איננו יותר נפלא מכח החכמה הנראית ביצירת הנמלה לפי קטנותה. אך כל אשר תקטן היצירה יהיה כח החכמה והיכולת נראה בה יותר ותקון הבורא יותר נפלא,

ונראה ממנה וזה יורה כי כולם מחשבות חושב אחד ובורא אחד מפני שהם מתדמים ושוים ונכונים להשלמת סדר העולם והעמדתו כלו בכל חלקיו ואלו היה לו יותר מבורא אחד היתה צורת החכמה מתחלפת כקצת חלקיו ולא היה צריך קצתו אל קצתו ומפני שהוא חלוק בשרשיו ויסודותיו שוה בתולדותיו ומחברותיו תראה כי מחדשו ומחברו ומנהיגו וחושבו אחד.

ואמר הפילוסוף אין במה שברא האלהים יותר נפלא ממה שברא ורצה לומר כי החכמה בקטן ובגדול מחלקי העולם מתדמה ושוה כמו שאמר דוד עליו השלום בספרי מיני ענייני העולם ותכונת ישובו (תהלים קד) מה רבו מעשיך ה' כלם בחכמה עשית מלאה הארץ קנינך ואמר (שם צב) מה גדלו מעשיך ה' מאד עמקו מחשבותיך:

והשלישי מפני החדוש הכולל את כל העולם כי הראיות למדו על חדושו. והוצרך בעבור זה שהיה לו מחדש מפני המנע הוית הדבר מאליו וכשאנו מוצאים הויה ויתברר לנו כי היה אחר שלא היה. נדע בעדות השכל השלם שזולתו בראו והמציא הויתו ויצר אותו,

וכיון שהתקיים כי לעולם בורא שבראו וחדשו אין ראוי להעלות על דעתנו שהוא יותר או פחות מאחד שאי אפשר למציאות העולם מבלי בורא אחד ואלו היה אפשר שיעלה בדעתנו שיתקיים העולם בפחות מבורא אחר היינו מעלים על דעתנו כן אך מפני שלא יכולנו להשכיל להשכיל דבר שיוכל לעשותו זולתו פחות מאחד ידענו ידיעה שאי אפשר לדחותה כי הוא אחד כי הדברים אשר יתבררו מצד הבאת הראיה עליהם ותהיה מציאותם מציאה שא"א לדחותה אין אנו צריכין להעלות על דעתנו שהם יותר ממה שהצורך מביא אליו בהשלמת הדבר שהוא לראיה עליהם.

והדמיון כי בעת שנראה כתב שוה בחבורו וצורות המכתב אשר נכתב בו צורה

~~ פרק ז ~~

אך הראיה שהבורא יתברך הוא אחד. הוא מפני שנתברר לנו בדרך הראיות כי יש
לעולם בורא. התחייבנו לחקור עליו אם הוא אחד או יותר מאחד. וצריך שנבאר
אמתת אחדותו משבעה פנים:

האחד מהם מצד בחינתנו לעילות הנמצאות כי כאשר נתבונן בהן נמצא מספרן
פחות מעלוליהן וכל אשר נחקור על עילות העילות ההן למעלה נמצא מספרן
פחות מהן וכל אשר תעלינה יתמעט מספרן עד שיגיע אל עילה אחת והיא עילת
העילות.

וביאור זה כי כי אישי הנמצאים אין תכלית למספרם. וכאשר נתבונן במיניהם
הכוללים אותם יהי' מספרם פחות מן האישים אשר תחתיהם. כי כל מין מן
המינים כולל אישים רבים והמינים יש תכלית למספרם. וכאשר נערוך המינים אל
סוגיהם הכוללים אותם יהיה מספר הסוגים פחות ממספרם כי תחת כל סוג
מהסוגים מינים רבים וכל אשר יעלו יהיה מספר הסוגים פחות עד אשר יגיעו אל
סוגי הסוגים.

וכבר אמר הפילוסוף כי סוגי הסוגים הם עשרה והם עצם וכמה ואיך ומצטרף
ואנה ומתי ומצב וקנין ופועל ונפעל,

וכאשר נחקור על עילות אישי מיני עשרת הסוגים האלה נמצאם חמש.

התנועה והיסודות הארבעה שהם האש והרוח והמים והעפר. וכאשר נחקור על
עילות היסודות הארבעה נמצאם החומר והצורה והם שנים. וכאשר נחקור על
עילתם יהיה מספרם פחות מהם והוא רצון הבורא יתברך ואין מספר פחות
משנים אלא אחד א"כ הבורא יתברך אחד על כל פנים,

וכן אמר דוד עליו השלום (ד"ה א כט) לך ה' הממלכה והמתנשא לכל לראש וגו'
ר"ל כי הוא רם על כל רמים ועליון על כל העליונים וראש כל תחלה ועילת כל
עילה ועלול:

והשני מצד סימני החכמה הנראים בכל העולם הזה עליונו ותחתונו קפאיו וצמחיו
ובעלי חיים אשר בו,

וכאשר נשתכל בו יורנו כי כלו מחשבת חושב אחד ומלאכת בורא אחד והוא שאנו
מוצאים אותו על מחלקותיו בשרשיו ויסודותיו מתדמה בתולדותיו ושוה בחלקיו
ואותות חכמת הבורא יתעלה נראות בקטני היצירות וגדוליה מעידות כי הם
לבורא א' חכם ואלו היה לעולם יותר מבורא אחד היתה צורת החכמה מתחלפת
בחלקי העולם ומשתנת בכלליו ובחלקיו.

סימן לחכמה וליכולת. והלא תראה אם ישפך לאדם דיו פתאום על נייר חלק
שא"א שיצטייר ממנו עליו כתב מסודר ושיטות נקראות כמו שיהיה בקולמוס. ואלו
הביא אדם לפנינו כתב מסודר ממה שאי אפשר להיות מבלי מצוע קולמוס ואומר
כי נשפך הדיו על הנייר ונעשתה צורת הכתב עליו מעצמה היינו ממהרים להכזיבו
על פניו שאיננו נמלט מכוונת מכוין,

וכיון שזה בעינינו דבר שא"א להיות בצורות רשומות בהסכמת דעתנו איך יוכל
לומר בדבר שמלאכתו יותר דקה ותקונו יותר רחוק ועמוק בעניננו עד אין תכלית
שיהיה מבלי כוונת מכוין וחכמת חכם ויכולת יכול'

וכל מה שהביאונו להעמיד מציאות הבורא יתעלה מצג מעשיו די למי שיבין ויודה
על האמת ומספיק בתשובת אנשי הקדמות שאומרים כי העולם קדמון ודחיית
דבריהם ואתה דע לך:

וכאשר נחקור על היסודות הארבעה נמצאם מחוברים מחומר וצורה והמה העצם
והמקרה,

והחומר שלהם הוא החומר הראשון אשר הוא שרש היסודות הארבעה והחומר
וההיולי שלהם.

והצורה היא הצורה הראשונה הכללית אשר היא שורש כל צורה עצמית וכל צורה
מקרית כחום וכקור וכלחות וכיובש והכובד והקלות והתנועה והמנוחה והדומה
להם,

וההרכבה והחבור נראים בכל העולם ובכל חלקיו בשרשיו ובענפיו בפשוטו
ובמורכבו בעליונו ובתחתונו וצריך ממה שהקדמנו שיהיה כולו מחודש כאשר
התברר לנו כי כל מחובר מחודש והדין חייב שנאמין כי העולם מחודש. וכיון שכן
הוא ונמנע שיהיה הדבר עושה את עצמו. צריך שיהיה לעולם עושה שהתחילו
וחדשו.

ומפני שהתברר כי ההתחלות א״א שיהיו מאין תכלית לתחלתם. מן הדין שיהיה
לעולם תחלה אין תחלה לפניו וראשון שאין לו ראשון. והוא אשר יצרו וחדשו מאין
דבר לא בדבר ולא על דבר,

וכמ״ש הכתוב בעניו הזה (ישעיה מד) אנכי ה׳ עושה כל נוטה שמים לבדי רוקע
הארץ מיאתי ואמר (איוב כו) נוטה צפון על תהו תולה ארץ על בלימה והוא הבורא
יתעלה אשר אותו דרשנו ולמצאו כווננו במחשבותינו ושכלנו. הוא הקדמון הראשון
אשר אין ראשית לראשיתו ואין תכלית לקדמותו כמו שאמר הכתוב (ישעיה מד) אני
ראשון ואני אחרון ואמר (שם מא) אני ה׳ ראשון ואת אחרונים אני הוא.

ויש בני אדם שאמרו שהעולם נהיה במקרה מבלי בורא שהתחילו ויוצר שיצרו ומן
התימה בעיני איך תעלה בדעת מדבר בעודנו בבריאותו כמחשבה הזאת ואלו
היה בעל המאמר הזה שומע אדם שיאמר במאמרו בגלגל אחד של מים שהוא
מתגלגל להשקות חלקה אחת של שדה או גנה וחושב כי זה נתקן מבלי כוונת
אומן שטרח בחבורו והרכבתו ושם כל כלי מכליו לעומת התועלת היה לו להפליא
ולהגדיל הרבה עליו ולחשוב אותו בתכלית הסכלות וימהר להכזיבו ולדחות
מאמרו וכיון שידחה המאמר הזה בגלגל קטן ופחות ונבזה שנעשה בתחבולה
קטנה לתקנת חלקה קטנה מהארץ איך יתיר לעצמו לחשוב כמחשבה הזאת
בגלגל הגדול הסובב את כל הארץ וכל אשר עליה מן הברואים. והוא בחכמה.
תקצרנה דעות כל בשר ושכלי המדברים להשיג היותה והוא מוכן לתועלת כל
הארץ וכל אשר עליה ואיך יוכל לומר שיהיה מבלי כונת מכוין ומחשבת חכם בעל
יכולת.

ומן הידוע אצלנו כי הדברים אשר הם מבלי כונת מכוין לא ימצא במאומה מהם

~~ פרק ו ~~

אך על איזה פנים נשתמש בההקדמות אשר זכרנו כברור מציאות הבורא יתעלה הוא.

כאשר נשתכל בעולם הזה נמצאהו מחובר ומורכב אין חלק מחלקיו מבלי חבור וסדור כי אנחנו רואים אותו בהרגשותינו ושכלנו כבית הבנוי אשר זומן בו כל הצריך לו. השמים ממעל כתקרה והארץ מתחת (ס"א מתוחה) כמצע והכוכבים מסודרים כנרות וכל הגופות צבורות בו כמכמנים כל דבר למה שצריך לו והאדם כבעל הבית המשתמש בכל אשר בו. ומיני הצמחים מזומנים לתועלתו ומיני החיות משתמשים להנאתו כמו שאמר דוד עליו השלום (תהלים ח) תמשילהו במעשי ידיך כל שתה תחת רגליו צנה ואלפים כלם וגם בהמות שדי צפור שמים ודגי הים עובר ארחות ימים.

וסדר זריחת השמש ובואה להעמיד עתי היום והלילה ועליתה וירידתה להמציא הקור והחום והקיץ והחורף מעניני הזמנים ותועלותיהם ושנותם תמיד על סדור א' מבלי הפסק כדכתיב (איוב ט) האומר לחרס ולא יזרח ובעד כוכבים יחתום וכתיב (תהלים קד) תשת חשך ויהי לילה וגו'.

וסבוב הגלגלים אשר תנועותם מתחלפות והכוכבים והמזלות על הנהגה משוערת ומשקל מכוון לא יזח ולא ישתנה והכוונה בכל דבר ממנו כוונת תועלת ותקנה למדברים כמו שאמר שלמה ע"ה (קהלת ג) את הכל עשה יפה בעתו גם את העולם נתן בלבם וגו' ואמר לכל זמן ועת לכל חפץ תחת השמים,

וכל זה חבורו והרכבתו נראים בכלו ובמקצתו וכשנעיין בצמחים ובבעלי חיים נמצאם מחוברים מהיסודות הארבעה והם האש והרוח והמים והעפר והמה נחלקים ונפרדים,

ואין בנו יכולת לחברם החבור הטבעי מפני שמקצתם משתנה אל קצתם וקצתם כנגד קצתם ואם נחבר דבר מהם הם ממהרים להשתנות ולהתחלף. אך החבור שחברה אותו התולדה הוא חבור מתוקן וקיים עד עת קץ.

וכבר חשבו קצת הפילוסופים כי הגלגלים והכוכבים והאישים העליונים הם מתולדת האש. ודומה לזה מ"ש דוד ע"ה (תהלים קד) עושה מלאכיו רוחות משרתיו אש לוהט ובזה ראיה על המחשבה הזאת ואיננה תולדה חמישית כאשר חשב אריסט"ו.

וכיון שהנמצאות הווות מן היסודות ומחוברות מהם וידענו כי לא נמזגו מאליהן ולא נתחברו בטבען מפני המחלוקת שביניהם עלו בדעתנו ונתברר בנפשותינו כי מחברם זולתם וקושרם בלעדיהם ומרכיבם כנגד טבעם על כרחם. הוא בוראם ית' אשר תקן קשורם ותכן חבורם.

לתחלתם.

ועוד מן הידוע כי כל מה שיש לו חלק יש לו כל כי אין הכל כי אם כלל חלקיו ולא יתכן להיות חלק למה שאין לו תכלית כי גדר החלק אינו כי אם שיעור נפרד משיעור כי שיעור הקטן סופר את הגדול כאשר זכר אקליד"ס בתחלת המאמר החמישי מספר השיעור.

ואם נעלה במחשבתנו דבר שאין לו תכלית בפועל ונפריש ממנו קצתו יהיה הנשאר פחות ממה שהיה קודם מבלי ספק ואם יהיה השאר מאין תכלית יהיה דבר שאין לו תכלית גדול מדבר שאין לו תכלית והוא מה שא"א.

ואם יהיה לשאר תכלית אם נוסיף עליו החלק המופרש ממנו והוא יש לו תכלית יהיה הכל דבר שיש לו תכלית. וכבר היה בתחלת דברינו מאין תכלית. וא"כ יהיה בתכלית ומאין תכלית וזה הפך שא"א להיות ולא יתכן להפריש ממה שאין לו תכלית חלק כי כל מה שיש לו חלק יש לו תכלית מבלי ספק,

וכשנחלק ממה שיצא אל גדר ההויה בעולם מן האישים מימי נח עד ימי משה ע"ה במחשבתנו יהיה חלק מכל אישי העולם והוא מגיע עד תכלית א"כ הכל הוא מגיע אל תכלית מספר. וכיון שכל העה"ז מגיע עד תכלית צריך שיהיו תחלותיו מגיעות עד תכלית מספר והדין נותן שיהיה לעולם הזה ראשון אין לפניו וצריך בעבור זה להגיע התחלות בראשיתם כאשר הקדמנו:

ובירור ההקדמה השלישית שנאמר כי כל מחובר מורכב מבלי ספק מדברים יותר מאחד והדברים ההם אשר חובר מהם הם קודמים לו הקדמה טבעית וכן צריך שיהיה מחברו קודם לו הקדמה זמנית וטבעית,

והקדמון הוא שאין לו עילה ומה שאין לו עילה אין לו תחלה ומה שאין לו תחלה אין לו תכלה ומה שיש לו תחלה איננו קדמון וכל מה שאינו קדמון הוא מחודש מפני שאין. בין הקדמון והמחודש אמצעי שיהיה לא קדמון ולא מחודש א"כ כל מחובר איננו קדמון ועל כל פנים הוא מחודש וכיון שנתבררה ההקדמה השלישית אשר זכרנו נתקיימו השלש הקדמות:

~~ פרק ה ~~

אך ההקדמות אשר יתברר מהן כי יש לעולם הזה בורא בראו מאין הן שלש הקדמות.

אחת מהנה כי הדבר אינו עושה את עצמו.

והשנית כי ההתחלות יש תכלית למספרן וכיון שיש תכלית למספרן יש להן ראשון שאין ראשון לפניו.

והשלישי כי כל מחובר מחודש.

וכאשר תתקיימנה אלה השלש הקדמות תהיה התולדה מהן למי שידע להשתמש בהן ולחברן כי יש לעולם בורא בראו מאין כמו שיתבאר ממה שאנו עתידין לבארו בע״ה.

והראיה על בירור אלו הג׳ הקדמות הוא מה שאספר.

והוא שנאמר כי כל נמצא אחר שלא היה איננו נמלט מאחד משני דברים אם שהמציא הוא את עצמו או שהמציא אותו זולתו.

וכל מה שנחשוב עליו שהוא עשה א״ע לא ימלט ג״כ מא׳ משני דברים אם שעשה א״ע קודם הויתו או אחר הויתו,

ושניהם אי אפשר כי אם נאמר שעשה א״ע אחר הויתו לא עשה כלום שלא היה צריך לעשות עצמו מפני הקדמת הויתו למעשהו א״כ לא עשה כלום.

ואם נאמר שעשה את עצמו קודם הויתו בעת ההיא היה אפס ואופס והאפס לא יהיה ממנו מעשה ולא הנחה כי האפס לא יעשה דבר ונמנע שיהיה הדבר עושה את עצמו בשום פנים,

והתבררה ההקדמה הראשונה אשר הקדמנו:

ובירור ההקדמה השנית הוא על הדרך הזה,

שכל מה שיש לו תכלה יש לו תחלה כי כבר נתברר שכל מה שאין לו תחלה אין לו תכלה מפני שא״א להגיע בדבר שאין לו תחלה אל גבול שיעמוד האדם אצלו,

ומה שנמצא לו אחרית נדע כי הוא לו היה לו ראשון אין ראשון לפניו ותחלה שאין לו תחלה וכל אשר נעמוד על תכלית מהההתחלות הנמצאות בעולם נדע כי היה להם ראשון אין ראשון לפניו ותחלה שאין לה תחלה. כי אין התחלות מבלי תכלית

~~ פרק ד ~~

אך איך דרך המחקר על אמתת היחוד ומה שאנו צריכין לדעתו קודם שנחקור על
היחוד אומר,

כי כל דבר שמבקשים לדעת אותו כשמסתפקים במציאותו צריך לשאול עליו
תחלה אם הוא נמצא אם לא וכשתתברר אמתת מציאותו צריך לחקור עליו מהו
ואיך הוא ולמה הוא. אך הבורא יתעלה אין אדם רשאי לשאול עליו אלא באם הוא
בלבד. וכשתתברר מציאותו בדרך העיון נחקור עליו אם הוא אחד או יותר מאחד.
וכאשר יתברר לנו שהוא אחד נחקור על ענין האחד ועל כמה פנים יאמר אחד
ובזה יתקיים לנו היחוד השלם כמו שאמר הכתוב (דברים ו) שמע ישראל ה' אלהינו
ה' אחד.

על כן אנחנו חייבים לחקור תחלה היש לעוה"ז בורא אם לא. וכאשר יתברר לנו
שיש לעולם בורא בראו וחדשו נחקור עליו אם הוא אחד או יותר מאחד וכשיתברר
כי הוא אחד נחקור על ענין האחד העובר והאחד האמת. ומה שצריך לספר בו על
הבורא מעניינו ובו ישלם ענין היחוד בלבנו ויגמר במחשבתנו בעז"ה:

~~ פרק ג ~~

אך לדעת אם אנו חייבין לחקור על היחוד בדרך העיון אם לא, אומר, כי כל מי שיוכל לחקור על הענין הזה והדומה לו מן הענינים המושכלים בדרך הסברא השכלית חייב לחקור עליו כפי השגתו וכח הכרתו.

וכבר הקדמתי בתחלת הספר הזה מן הדברים המראים חיוב הענין מה שיש בו די והמתעלם מחקור הרי זה מגונה ונחשב מן המקצרים בחכמה ובמעשה והוא דומה לחולה שהוא בקי בחליו ובדרך רפואתו סמך על רופא שמרפא אותו בכמה מיני רפואות והוא מתעצל לעיין בחכמתו וסברתו ברפואות הרופא לדעת אם הוא מתעסק בעניניו על דרך נכונה אם לא והיה יכול לעמוד על זה מבלי דבר שימנעהו. וכבר חייבתנו התורה בזה כמו שכתוב (שם) וידעת היום והשבות אל לבבך וגו'.

והראיה שהמחשבה אל הלב הוא עיון השכל הוא מה שאמר הכתוב (ישעיה מד) ולא ישיב אל לבו ולא דעת ולא תבונה וגו' ואמר דוד המלך ע"ה (דה"א כח) ואתה שלמה בני דע את אלהי אביך ועבדהו בלב שלם ובנפש חפצה כי כל לבבות דורש ה' וגו'

ואמר (תהלים ק) דעו כי ה' הוא האלהים וגו'

ואמר (שם נא) אשגבהו כי ידע שמי ואמר (ירמיה ט) כי אם בזאת יתהלל המתהלל השכל וידוע אותי ואמרו רבותינו ז"ל הוי שקוד ללמוד תורה ודע מה שתשיב לאפיקורוס ואמרה תורה (דברים ד) ושמרתם ועשיתם כי היא חכמתכם ובינתכם לעיני העמים וגו'

וא"א שיודו לנו האומות במעלות החכמה והבינה עד שיעידו לנו הראיות והמופתים ועדי השכל על אמתת תורתנו ואומן אמונתנו. וכבר הבטיחנו יוצרנו לגלות מסך הסכלות מעל שכלם ושיראה כבודו הבהיר לאות לנו על אמתת תורתנו כאשר אמר (ישעיה ס) והלכו גוים לאורך וגו' ואומר (שם ב) והלכו עמים רבים ואמרו לכו ונעלה אל הר ה' וגו'.

וכבר התבאר מן השכל ומן הכתוב ומן הקבלה שאנו חייבין לעיין במה שנוכל להשיג בירורו בדעתנו:

העיר אשר שם מגמתו אליה אע"פ שהוא יודע אותו הצד ואותה הפאה,

והוא יגע למאד ואיננו מגיע אל חפצו מפני שאינו יודע הדרך כמו שאמר הכתוב (קהלת י) עמל הכסילים תיגענו אשר לא ידע ללכת אל עיר.

והחלק הרביעי הוא יחוד האלהים בלב ובלשון אחר אשר ידע להביא הראיות עליו ולעמוד על אמתת אחדותו מדרך העיון והסברות הנכונות השכליות וזהו החלק השלם והחשוב שבהם והמעלה הזאת היא אשר הזהיר עליה הנביא באמרו (דברים ד) וידעת היום והשבות אל לבבך כי ה' הוא האלהים וגומר:

~~ פרק ב ~~

אמר המחבר אך על כמה פנים מתחלק יחוד הבורא. אומר. מפני שפשטה מלת
יחוד בדברי אנשי היחוד הרגילו בה הרבה בלשונם ובמלותם תמיד עד אשר שבה
אצלם ממלות התימה על הטוב ועל הרע,

והם משתמשים בה בחרדתם לצרה גדולה להגדילה ולהפליא ענינה ואינם מעלים
על מחשבתם להבין אמתת ענין מה שיעבירו על לשונם מן הסכלות והעצלות והם
חושבים כי ענין היחוד נגמר להם כאשר נגמרה מלתו ולא ירגישו כי לבותם ריקים
מאמתתו ומצפוניהם נעורים מעניינו מפני שמיחדים אותו בלשונם ובמלתיהם
ויחשבוהו בלבבם יותר מהאחד במצפונם בדמות שאר האחדים הנמצאים
ויספרו אותו במדות לא תאותנה לאחד האמת בעבור שאינם יודעים ענין האחד
האמת וענין האחד האחד העובר אלא הסגולה מאנשי היחוד שהעמיקו בחכמה והבינו
ענין הבורא והנברא וחוקי האחד האמת ומה שהוא מתבודד בו.

ואמת אמר הפילוסוף באמרו לא יוכל לעבוד עילת העילות ותחלת ההתחלות אלא
נביא הדור בטבעו או הפילוסוף המובהק במת שקנהו מן החכמה אבל זולתם,
עובדים זולתו, מפני שאינם מבינים נמצא אלא מורכב.

ובעבור זה מתחלק היחוד כפי התחלקות דעות בני אדם ויתרון הכרתם על
ארבעה חלקים:

תחלתם יחוד האל בלשון בלבד והמעלה הזאת היא המעלה אשר יגיע אליה
הקטן והפתי אשר איננו יודע ענין האמונה ואין אמתתה קבוע בלבו.

והחלק השני הוא יחוד האל בלב ובלשון ע"י הקבלה מפני שהוא מאמין במי
שקבל מהם ואיננו יודע אמתת הענין מצד שכלו ותבונתו והוא כעור הנמשך אחרי
פקח ואפשר שיקבל ממקבל כמותו והוא כחברת עורים שם כל אחד מהם ידו על
שכם חבירו עד שהגיעו אל הפקח אשר בראש החבורה שמנהיגם שאם יפשע
הפקח הזה בהם ויתעלם מהם ולא יזהר בשמירתם או אם יכשל אחד מהם או
יקרהו מקרה. יקרה לכל המקרה ההוא ויתעו מני דרך ואפשר שיפלו בבור או
בגומין או שיכשלו בדבר שימנעם מלכת.

וכן המיחד מצד הקבלה אין בוטחין בו שלא יבא לידי שיתוף שאם ישמע דברי
המשנים וטענותם אפשר שתשתנה דעתו ויטעה ולא יכיר ומפני זה אמרו רז"ל
הוי שקוד ללמוד תורה ודע מה שתשיב לאפיקורוס.

והחלק הג' מחלקי היחוד הוא יחוד הבורא בלב ובלשון אחר שיוכל להביא עליו
ראיות על אמתת מציאותו כדרך העיון מבלי דעת ענין האחד האמת והאחד
העובר. וזה דומה לפקח שהוא הולך בדרך והוא רוצה ללכת אל ארץ רחוקה
והדרך מתחלקת לדרכים רבים מסופקים ואיננו יודע ומכיר הדרך הנכונה אל

~~ פרק א ~~

אמר המחבר

בגדר יחוד האלהים בלב שלם הוא שיהיו הלב והלשון שוים ביחוד הבורא ית׳
אחר אשר יבין בדרכי הראיות בירור מציאותו ואמתת אחדותו מדרך העיון מפני
שיחוד האלהים מתחלק במדברים כפי התחלקות הכרתם והבנתם.

מהם מי שמיחד אותו בלשונו בלבד והוא שישמע ב״א אומרים דבר והוא נמשך
אחריהם מבלי דעת ענין מה שהוא אומר.

ומהם מי שמיחדהו בלבו ולשונו ויבין ענין מה שהוא אומר מדרך הקבלה שקבל
מאבותיו ואיננו יודע בירור מה שקבל מהענין ההוא.

ומהם מי שמיחדהו אחר שיבין מדרך הראיות אמתת הענין אך יחשבנו במחשבתו
כשאר האחדים הנמצאים ויבא להגשים הבורא ולהמשילהו בצורה ובדמות מפני
שאיננו יודע אמתת יחודו וענין מציאותו.

ומהם מי שמיחדהו בלבו ולשונו אחר שיבין ענין האחד האמת והאחד העובר
ויביא ראיות על ברור מציאותו ואמתת יחודו וזהו החלק השלם בענין היחוד.

על כן אמרתי בגדר היחוד השלם שהוא השוואת הלב והלשון ביחוד הבורא אחר
שידע להביא ראיה עליו ולדעת אופני אמתת אחדותו מדרך העיון:

והשביעי להביא ראיות שהוא אחד

והשמיני לבאר עניני האחד העובר והאחד האמת

והתשיעי שהאל יתברך אחד אמת ואין אחד אמת זולתו

והעשירי במדות האלהיות המושכלות והכתובות והפנים אשר יתבאר מהם
לקיימם לו ולהרחיקם ממנו:

וכל זה להזהיר על מה שהקדים במאמר והיו הדברים האלה אשר אנכי מצוך היום על-לבבך שתהיה רגילות לשונו בהם תמיד מביאה לידי זכרון הלב ולא יפנה לבבו מזכור האלהים תמיד. וזה דומה למה שאמר דוד המלך ע"ה (תהלים טז) שויתי ה' לנגדי תמיד ואמר הכתוב (דברים ל) כי קרוב אליך הדבר מאד בפיך ובלבבך לעשותו.

ואחר כן נעתק מחובות האברים אל מה שיש בו מעשה בלבד ושמהו ג' חלקים באמרו וקשרתם לאות על ידך והיו לטוטפות בין עיניך וכתבתם על מזוזות ביתך ובשעריך והם תפלה של יד ותפלה של ראש והמזוזה וכלם גורמים לזכור את הבורא ולאהבו בלב שלם ולכסוף לו וכמו שאמר הכתוב בחקי זכרון אהבת האוהבים (שיר השירים ח) שימני כחותם על לבך כחותם על זרועך וגומר ואמר (שם א) צרור המור דודי לי בין שדי ילין. ושם אותם שלשה כדי שיהיו חזקים וקיימים יותר כאשר אמר החכם (קהלת ו) והחוט המשלש לא במהרה ינתק.

והפרק הזה כולל עשרה ענינים חמשה מהם רוחניים וחמשה מהם גשמיים.

והרוחניים תחלתם שהבורא נמצא והב' שהוא אלהינו והג' שהוא אחד והד' שנאהבהו והחמישי שנאהב אותו בלב שלם.

והחמשה הגשמיים תחלתם ושננתם והשני ודברת בם והשלישי וקשרתם לאות וגו' והרביעי והיו לטוטפות וגו' והחמישי וכתבתם על מזוזת וגו'.

וארז"ל למה קדמה שמע לוהיה אם שמוע כדי שיקבל עליו עול מלכות שמים תחלה ואחר כך יקבל עליו עול מצות. ועל כן ראיתי להקדים שער היחוד על שאר שערי הספר הזה.

וצריך שאבאר עתה מענין היחוד בלב שלם עשרה ענינים.

הראשון מה גדר היחוד בלב שלם

והשני על כמה חלקים מתחלק ענין היחוד

והשלישי אם נתחייב לחקור עליו בדרך העיון אם לא

והרביעי איך דרך מחקרו ומה אנו צריכין לדעת תחלה קודם שנחקור על היחוד

והחמישי לברר ההקדמות אשר יתברר מהן כי יש לעולם בורא בראו מאין

והששי היאך נביאם לקיים מציאות הבורא

‎~~~ חובות הלבבות - שער היחוד ~~~

‎~~ הקדמה ~~

בבאור אופני חיוב יחוד האל יתברך בלב שלם. וזה פתח השער:
אמר המחבר כאשר חקרנו על מה שהצורך אליו יותר מפנות דתנו ושרשיה מצאנו
יחוד האלהים בלב שלם שרשה ויסודה שהוא השער הראשון משערי התורה
וביחוד יפרד המאמין מן הכופר והוא ראש אמתת הדת. ומי שנטה ממנו לא יתכן
לא מעשה ולא תתקיים לו אמונה.

ומפני זה היה תחלת דברי האלהים אלינו על הר סיני (שמות כ) אנכי ה׳ אלהיך לא
יהיה לך אלהים אחרים וגו׳ והזהירנו אחר כן על יד נביאו באמרו (דברים ו) שמע
ישראל ה׳ אלהינו ה׳ אחד.

וצריך שתבין הפרק הזה של שמע ישראל עד סופו ותראה היאך נעתקו בו דבריו
מענין לענין וכלל עשרה ענינים כנגד עשרת הדברות,

והוא שצונו להאמין בבורא יתברך באמרו שמע ישראל ה׳. ולא התכוון בכאן
באמרו שמע לשמע האזן אך התכוון לאמונת הלב כמו שאמר הכתוב (שמות כד)
נעשה ונשמע (דברים ו) ושמעת ישראל ושמרת לעשות וגו׳ וכל מה שבא על הדרך
הזה בלשון שמיעה לא התכוון בו כי אם להאמין ולקבל.

ואחרי אשר חייבנו להאמין באמתת מציאותו חייבנו להאמין שהוא אלהינו כמו
שאמר אלהינו ואחר כן חייבנו להאמין כי הוא אחד אמת כמו שאמר ה׳ אחד.

ואחר שחייבנו להאמין ולקבל שלשה הענינים האלה אשר זכרנו מהם נעתק אל
מה שאנו חייבין לחבר אליהם והוא אהבת האל בלב שלם בסתר ובגלוי בנפשנו
ובמאודנו כמו שאמר (שם) ואהבת את ה׳ אלהיך בכל לבבך ובכל נפשך ובכל
מאדך ואני עתיד לבאר הענין הזה בשער אהבת האל בעזר הצור.

ואחר כן נעתק מהם להזהיר על חובות הלבבות באמרו והיו הדברים האלה אשר
אנכי מצוך היום על לבבך ר״ל שתתדביקם אל לבך ותאמין בם במצפונך.

ואחר כן נעתק מהם אל מצות האברים שהם כוללים הידיעה והעשיה כמו שנאמר
ושננתם לבניך,

ודברת בם שאם לא יהיה לך אל בן תשים הבן עילת קריאתך אותם.

ואחר כן אמר בשבתך בביתך ובלכתך בדרך ובשכבך ובקומך שאין נמנע מן הלב
ומן הלשון מה שהם חייבין בו כמו שאפשר לנמנע משאר האברים כאשר הקדמנו
חיוב מצות הלבבות תדיר בפתיחת הספר הזה.

SOME OTHER WORKS BY RABBI YOSEF SEBAG

Pirkei Avot — www.dafyomireview.com/489

Duties of the Heart — www.dafyomireview.com/384

Path of the Just — www.dafyomireview.com/447

Gates of Holiness — www.dafyomireview.com/442

Marks of Divine Wisdom — www.dafyomireview.com/427

Torah Authenticity — www.dafyomireview.com/430

yosefsebag@gmail.com